700
Sundays

BY BILLY CRYSTAL

WARNER BOOKS

LARGE PRINT

Studio photography by Andrew Eccles.

Milt Gabler and Commodore Music Shop photo on page 39 courtesy of Don Peterson.

Warner Books

Time Warner Book Group
1271 Avenue of the Americas, New York, NY 10020
Visit our Web site at www.twbookmark.com.

Printed in the United States of America

First Edition: October 2005
10 9 8 7 6 5 4 3 2 1

ISBN: 0-446-57879-7 (Large Print Edition)
LCCN: 2005932416

The Large Print Edition published in accord with the standards of the N.A.V.H.

For Mom and Dad

ACKNOWLEDGMENTS

Creating and performing *700 Sundays* on Broadway was the most fulfilling time in my career. Many people helped make that journey the joy it was, and in many ways also made this book possible. So, to Des McAnuff, who directed the play, and to my collaborator and friend Alan Zweibel for his work, some of which graces these pages. I thank you.

To two David Steinbergs. One, my manager, who encouraged me to get back on stage. And the other David Steinberg, the comedian, who literally was on stage with me. To David Letterman, whose show became a safe place to go out and be funny. To Robin Williams, who always encouraged me to get back up there. To everyone at Warner Books and Jennifer Joel at ICM who has embraced the writing, and to the audiences at the La Jolla Playhouse in California and the Broadhurst on Broadway that were so extraordinary. To Steve and Andrew Tenenbaum, Larry Brezner, and Larry Magid, for all they have done.

To all my relatives, some long gone, I'm so grateful for your love and laughter. To Jenny, Michael, Ella, and Lindsay for their devotion, and to my brothers Joel and Rip, who were always up there with me. And to Janice: Did you ever think when we first met, that some day we would be on stage together at Radio Music Hall, Tony awards in our hands, standing in front of our kids? "Can you dig that? I knew that you could."

—bc

700
Sundays

"Consider the rose . . . The rose is the sweetest smelling flower of all, and it's the most beautiful because it's the most simple, right? But sometimes, you got to clip the rose. You got to cut the rose back, so something sweeter smelling and stronger, and even more beautiful, will grow in its place."

—Zutty Singleton

1957: We got a new car

CHAPTER 1

*W*e got a new car!

I was the most excited kid in the world because we finally got a new car, and I didn't even know what make it was. All my father said on the phone was, "I just bought a new car, and it's a surprise, so, everybody be out in front of the house because I'm going to pull up exactly at noon." So right before noon, we stood in the driveway, my brothers, my mom and I, trying to guess what Dad bought.

3

"Maybe it's the Ford Fairlane," Joel, who was fifteen, wondered.

"No, I bet it's the Bonneville," Rip, eleven, said with authority.

"He mentioned something about the Chrysler Imperial," said Mom.

I interrupted, which I always did because I was the youngest and the shortest, which made me the loudest. I was also nine. "Wait, he said it was a surprise! What if he got," as I looked up to the sky with hope, "a *Cadillac*?" (I swear I could hear angels singing.)

We were silent for a brief moment, all of us considering that heavenly possibility, when we heard Pop's honk, and there he was waving, as he pulled up in our brand-new, right-out-of-the-showroom, 1957 . . . gray-on-gray Plymouth Belvedere.

What the hell was he thinking? Of all the cool cars out there, he picks *this* one? A Plymouth? And gray? Gray isn't even its own color, it's a combination of black and white. And two tones of it?

This was not the car of my dreams, but at least it was a new car with big fins, red leather interior and push-button transmission. The Plymouth replaced the only car I ever knew in my life and I was glad to see this car go. It was an embarrassing-to-drive-around-Long-Beach-in big, black, boxy, 1948 Chevrolet. This was an ugly automobile. It had a sun visor over the front windshield, so it looked like the car was wearing a fedora. Sometimes it looked like the car was an old-time film noir detective sitting in front of our house. It wasn't a family car. This was a getaway car. They killed Sonny on the Causeway in this car. Why on earth would he keep this car for nine years?

Two reasons. One, we couldn't afford anything else; and two, my father loved this car. He took perfect care of this car. He even named the car. He named the car "Nellie." Men always name their cars after women, and talk about them like they are women. It's always, "She's a beauty, isn't she?" It's never, "Isn't Ira a great-looking car?" Boats are almost always named after wives, daughters, or girlfriends. I have never seen the SS *Larry*. Even the man who dropped the bomb on Hiroshima named the plane after his mother, *Enola Gay*:

"Hi Mom, I just dropped the A-bomb on Japan and killed eighty thousand people, and I named the plane after you!"

"Oh son, thank you, I can't wait to call Ida, she's always bragging about her Sidney."

And men talk to their cars, just like they're women—"Come on girl, turn over baby, turn over." Men treat their

6

cars like women: put a lot of miles on them, and eventually they trade them in for newer models.

Toward the end of Nellie's life with us, she suffered from post-ignition syndrome or PIS, as Emily Dickinson called it. That meant you would turn off the ignition, and poor Nellie would sputter and spew for a few minutes afterward. It sounded like Nellie was an old woman getting in the last words in an argument:

"No, it's you. It's you. Not me. It's you. It's you. It's you. Not me. It's you. Not me. Not me. It's you. It's you. Not me. It's you. It's you. It's you. Not me. It's you. Not me. Not me. It's you. Not me. Not me. Fuck you!"

So finally we have the new car, with its intoxicating "new car smell," which smells exactly like . . . a new car. We took it out for a ride to celebrate at our

7

favorite Chinese restaurant in Long Beach—because it was the *only* Chinese restaurant in Long Beach—a place on Park Avenue that we loved, a place called Wing Loo.

We were sitting in the front booth, the picture window behind us, and my dad was in a giddy mood. He had a couple of vodka gimlets, which is vodka, with just a splash of gimlet in it. And every time Mr. Loo would go by, Dad would giggle and say, "What's new, Loo?" And the gray-on-gray Plymouth Belvedere was outside, gleaming under the streetlight, as best a gray-on-gray Plymouth Belvedere can. We were having the time of our lives. In other words, a perfect time for something to go wrong.

Big John Ormento was one of the local Mafiosos in Long Beach. There were a number of reputed gangsters living there. In fact in the book of *The*

Godfather, Vito Corleone and family lived in Long Beach. Big John was scary, our Luca Brasi. While we were eating our egg rolls, and drinking our drinks with the little umbrellas in them, we had no idea that Big John Ormento was drunk driving *his* new car, a 1957, anti-Semitic Lincoln Continental. And he came roaring up Park Avenue, swerved and slammed into the back of the Belvedere, which then slammed into the back of the car in front of it, reducing our new car to a 1957 gray-on-gray Plymouth Belv! The crash was tremendous. We turned around so fast lo mein flew out of our mouths hitting and sticking to the window.

Big John staggered out of his car, surveyed the damage, shook his head a few times and started to laugh.

"Oh my God, it's Big John," Mom gasped.

"I'm going out there," said Dad as he started to push his way out of the black leather booth.

"Don't, Jack, what if he has a gun?" Dad ordered another gimlet.

Ormento ran to his car and took off.

Ten minutes later, Officer Miller was questioning my father. "Did you see who did this, Mr. Crystal?"

Dad never hesitated. "No, we heard the crash, and by the time we got out here, they were gone."

Mom looked at Dad, confused a bit, but knowing he probably did the right thing. Joel and Rip and I were dying to tell, but "dying" being the operative word here, we said nothing.

"Some people," the cop muttered. "Must have been some kid going too fast."

"Yeah," said Pop. "These kids today . . ."

It was a Sunday night, and Dad's service station, "Stan's," was closing early. Stan told Dad he didn't have any room for the car in the shop, but he would tow it to our house and pick it up in the morning.

The twisted piece of metal sat in front of our house, at 549 East Park in Long Beach, Long Island. A sleepy beach town of approximately ten thousand people, which nodded off in the winter and woke up in July to three times as many enjoying a beautiful summer at the sea, Long Beach was surrounded by water. The bay (Reynold's Channel) on one side of town, with its beautiful wetlands; and the Atlantic Ocean on the other, its thunderous waves hitting the shore of beautiful white sand beaches. The boardwalk stretched the length of the town and featured some amusement park rides. There were games of chance, and a batting cage, a soft ice cream shop, a knish place (Izzy's) and a large municipal swimming pool. Modest homes, and the occasional thirties mansion, dotted the tree-lined streets. A few hotels near the boardwalk were once filled with people, making Long Beach at one time a sort of Atlantic City without the saltwater taffy and the diving horse. The abandoned submarine watch tower, left standing since World War II, was the place to take your girl for a kiss, or smoke a cigarette for the first time. At one time there was horseback riding on the beach, and supposedly George M. Cohan wrote "Only 45 Minutes from Broadway" about Long Beach.

It was known as America's healthiest city, which is why my sickly grandparents moved there from the Bronx and bought homes for my Uncle Danny and us, in 1951. It was a wonderful place to live. However, at nine o'clock that Monday morning, Long Beach didn't feel like the safest place to be.

Stunned, the five of us sat in the living room bemoaning the loss of the Belvedere. The doorbell rang and I got it. I always got the door because I thought someday somebody's going to be there who would take me to Hollywood.

When I opened the door, there was an overcoat, a neck and an eyebrow. Big John Ormento was in the doorway. He looked down at me, which wasn't difficult. I was surprised to see his face.

Usually gangsters like this are on television, sitting in silhouette confessing to their gruesome crimes, their voices electronically altered, sounding like Darth Vader on Quaaludes. Big

13

John's voice was deep—it actually seemed to echo—and he had an accent as thick as his police file.

"Can I see your father, please?"

My heart was beating so loud, I thought he could hear it. My throat was dry, making it a full octave higher than it already was.

"I will go and see if there is one here." And I ran into the living room, faster than a hyperactive midget wrestler.

"Dad, Big John Ormento's here. Big John Ormento's outside. He's going to kill us. He's going to kill all of us! We're doomed!"

"Billy, calm down. Calm down. He's not here to hurt us. He probably just wants to talk to me. Let him in."

"Me? I'm nine! I've got everything to live for!" (I became a better actor later.) "Please."

"Let him in."

I went back to the door to get Big John; he seemed even bigger, his head was so large it caused a total eclipse of the sun.

"Come on in." He followed me into the living room. He stood there, looking menacing, and uncomfortable. He stared at my dad, took off his hat, and then he spoke.

"Hey, how fast do think your car was going when it backed into my car?"

We all froze. Big John broke out in a Pavarotti kind of laugh. "I'm just kidding. How you doing? I'm John Ormento. Nice to meet you, Mr. Crystal, Mrs. Crystal, you boys here. Listen. I'm very sorry for what happened to your car last night. Very sorry. It was my fault, it was an accident, believe me, it was an accident. If it wasn't an accident, this would be a condolence call.

"I talked to my 'friends' and they

15

told me you didn't tell the cops nothing. So I want to make it up to yous."

"Okay, Mr. Ormento. I have my insurance card. We'll just put it through
the insurance company."

Big John interrupted Dad with an
impatient laugh, the same way he probably interrupted somebody who
wasn't beating up a guy properly. "No,
no, no, no. We're not going to do something stupid like put it through the insurance company, no. Cuz let's face it,
we *are* the insurance company!

"I want to do something special for
yous."

Dad looked confused. "What do
you mean 'special'?"

"I asked around about you, Mr.
Crystal. People like you. They respect
what you do, and they like your wife
and your boys here. Don't you think
you should be driving around in a car

that more befits a man of your altitude?"

We all looked confused.

"What are you trying to say, Mr. Ormento?"

"What I'm trying to say is this, Mr. Crystal. I want to buy you a new car, any car you want, the car of your choice."

Things were looking up! Any car we want? The car of our choice? Oh baby, I was overjoyed! All those great cars were now rolling around my brain, like a slot machine: the Impala, the Bel Air, the Thunderbird, the Corvette! Oh, a Corvette! *Think with me, Pop, think with me, Corvette, Corvette, Corvette,* I said to myself over and over, trying to send my message telepathically.

"Let's just get this car fixed," Dad said.

Shit! I said to myself.

17

Big John looked angry, and as he stepped forward, he got bigger.

"Let me ask you something, Mr. K . . ." I wanted to correct him, but I have this thing about dying. "You are refusing my offer? Huh? That upsets me. You know, that really upsets me, and it confuses me. Why would you not want me to buy you a new car?"

Dad stood tall and simply said, "Because, Mr. Ormento, *I* bought this one."

There was silence as they stared at each other. It got tense. Big John's shark eyes trying to intimidate, as they lasered into Dad's eyes, trying to push him to reconsider, and probably thinking, How can I get this guy's whole body into a can of tuna. Dad, only five foot nine and 160 pounds, just stared back at Big John, unafraid.

I looked at my mother. She looked at my father, and she smiled a smile of pride that I've never, ever forgotten.

She took one step over next to him, put her arm around Pop, and together the two of them smiled at Big John Ormento.

Those were my parents.

Two weeks later, the car came back. Well, Big John knew a lot about bodywork because the car looked great, and after we opened the trunk to make sure there were no bodies in it, we took it out for a ride. And everything was great until Dad tried to make a right turn. Almost impossible. The car barely reacted to Dad's turning of the steering wheel. It moaned and groaned; so did Dad. The car just couldn't make right turns very well. They couldn't fix that. You actually had to make three left turns in order to make one right turn. But it didn't matter; we had our new car.

They put me up front, in the middle,

with my brothers in the back. I sat up front because I was the one who didn't need legroom; and I still don't. I always sat in between my mom and my dad because my mom never drove the car when Dad was around . . . never. Dad was very much a man of the times. He was the hunter, gatherer, driver . . . er . . . But when we were sitting like this, she would always take her left arm and put it behind my head and let it rest lightly on the right shoulder of the man that she loved so much. And I would sit in the middle, and I would look at him, my first hero, as he drove that car, his left arm outside the window getting that little yarmulke tan around his elbow, and smoking his cigarette—because they told us in the fifties, "Cigarettes taste good and are so good for you." And he looked like he was driving a Rolls-Royce or a Bentley, never for once thinking he was driving a gray-on-gray Plymouth Belvedere that couldn't make right turns. That was my dad.

He worked so hard for us all the time. He held down two jobs, including weekend nights. The only day we really had alone with him was Sunday. Sunday was our day for my two brothers and I to put on a show and make them laugh. Sunday was our day to go up on the boardwalk in Long Beach and play Skeeball or Fascination, go to the batting cage, play baseball, go bowling, or to the movies, even a Broadway show. Sunday night was our night to go out to eat together. We'd always go out for Italian food, or Chinese food, because on Sunday nights, Jews are not allowed to eat their own food. That's in the Talmud.

"On the seventh day, God rested and then went to Twin Dragons for dinner, because He loved the ribs." If you go to any Italian restaurant on a Sunday, there are only Jewish families. If you go to a

21

Chinese restaurant, there are only Jewish families. Have you ever seen a Chinese family at a deli on a Sunday having a big plate of pickled herring, and chopped liver? It doesn't happen.

And Dad would come in like three, four o'clock on a Sunday morning after working all weekend. Just as the sun came up, I would tiptoe over to their bedroom, which was right next to my room in the back, and I would quietly open the door just a little, and there they would be, Mom and Dad, lying there, looking so quiet, and so peaceful together. And I would sit in the doorway waiting for him to wake up, just to see what we were going to do together that day. I just couldn't wait for Sundays. I couldn't wait for Sundays. He died suddenly when I was fifteen. I once calculated that I had roughly 700 Sundays. That's it. 700 Sundays. Not alot of time for a kid to have with his dad.

Birth

New Hep Cat

Jack Crystal, producer of jazz concerts and jazz record authority, welcomed a brand new son, William Edward, Sunday. This is the third Crystal son and gives Jack a potential hot trio.

Circumcision

CHAPTER 2

*S*unday Number One. I'm born.

Sunday, March 14, 1948, in Manhattan at Doctor's Hospital overlooking Gracie Mansion, 7:30 in the morning. They tell me that I was a rather difficult birth.

"Keep pushing, Helen. Baby's starting to come now. Here he comes, Helen. Keep pushing. How do you feel, Helen?"

"Fuck you. This hurts, that's how I feel."

"There it is. I can see the face. Oh, that's a cute-looking baby, Helen."

"Who does it look like?"

"Joe Louis, actually. Uh-oh. The baby's shoulders are too big for you. We need forceps to get the baby out of there."

Oh, my God! I saw the forceps coming toward me. I said, "You know what? I'll come back later, you're all so busy. Thanks anyway. I'll see you in a little while."

They pulled me out. Somebody slapped me on the ass. Pow! WAAAAAH! They put me on a cold scale. WAAAAH! The doctor sounded like the man behind the counter at the deli as he looks at the needle on the scale after he puts more than half a pound of corned beef on it . . .

"It's a little bit over. You still want it?"

Yes, a rather difficult birth, which

my relatives always reminded me about every time they saw me.

"Oh, there's the little guy who almost split his mother in two."

"Billy, don't take this personal, but your mother didn't sit down until you were twelve years old."

I didn't take it personal.

Sunday Number Two: my circumcision. This I took personal.

This is no way to be brought into the world. I'm on a pillow, totally naked, eight pounds, nine ounces. I looked like a boiled chicken. I'm brought out in front of the family by a guy with bad breath and a beard. He puts me down on a table, grabs a razor and my penis and cuts off the top . . . six to eight inches . . .

"Get me the electric knife. Stand back when I yell timber. Come on. Whoa. Look at that. That's a five-skin!

27

Look at the size of this thing! Hey, throw it on the car. It looks like it may rain."

I'm screaming in pain, "My dick, my dick!" and then I heard my Uncle Herman yell, "Let's eat!" Because, you find out, in Yiddish "bris" means blood and buffet.

Sunday Number Three. I got a gun. I was only two weeks old, but if somebody was coming near my dick again, they were going down.

Now you can't pick the family that you're born into. That's just the roll of the dice. It's just luck. But if I could pick these people, I would pick them over and over again because they were lunatics. Fun lunatics. What a crazy group of people, and great characters too. It was like the *Star Wars* bar, but everybody had accents.

Good people, immigrant people who came here and made something of themselves. There were two sides of our family, the Crystal side, and the Gabler side.

The Crystal side was small. It was Dad, his brother, Berns, and their sister, Marcia. There weren't that many cousins in his extended family. His mom, Sophie, was a sweet Russian woman. We actually look a great deal alike. She had left Kiev when she was just fifteen. Told her parents she was going to take a walk, and made her way to America.

My grandfather, Julius Crystal, died when my dad was just sixteen. He was a very interesting man. His immigration forms said he was also from Russia, but recent information has him from Finland. Julius had been an actor in the Yiddish theater. He translated *King Lear* into Yiddish and he played

29

Lear with Sophie playing Cordelia. He also wrote a book called *The Tyranny of God.* They lived for a while in Grand Rapids, Michigan, and moved to Brooklyn when Dad was around nine. I once asked Grandma Sophie, Why did they live in Grand Rapids? She said, "That's where the train stopped."

My Aunt Marcia was one of my favorites, a beautiful red-haired blue-eyed woman, with a great sense of humor. I always felt extremely close to her. Uncle Berns was the baby, all six foot four and 250 pounds of him. He was a true eccentric, bigger than life. He had the mime ability of a circus clown, and he could do magic tricks, and would always use one of us as his assistant. He seemed more like our older brother. He was the uncle you could play with. He was an artist, who had actually been ordered by Eisenhower during World War II to interpret the war on canvas. His first assignment was D-Day. His life story would later become a documentary film directed by my daughter Lindsay, for HBO.

The Gabler side was Mom's family. She was one of six brothers and sisters. The generation before them was a mixture of the Kasindorfs, from Rostov on the Don in Russia, and the Gablers of Vienna.

My Grandma Susie (Kasindorf) was one of nine children. Grandpa Julius (Gabler) was one of four brothers, and all of these people had a lot of kids; they really took the "Be fruitful and multiply" quote from the Bible very seriously. So when we all got together for a holiday dinner, it was an enormous crowd of colorful characters. There was my Aunt Lee, who was one of the first woman bank presidents in America; her brother, my Uncle Sid Kasindorf, who was an inventor. He actually built one of the first transistor radios; he put it in a box of wooden stick matches, and it was featured at the World's Fair of 1939. My Aunt Jean (Mom's sister) and Uncle Greenie were husband-and-wife doctors. Greenie wrote the first papers on ambulating patients after surgery. There were furriers and architects, accountants, a baby bonnet salesman, even a suspected spy.

Our Russian cousin Albert Parry (born Paretsky), who knew Lenin as a teenager, and had escaped his revolution after Lenin had told him how bloody the revolution would be, came to America, taught Russian Studies at Cornell University, wrote several controversial books on Russia and may have helped track down war criminals after World War II. We went to Russia together, when I did an HBO special there in 1989—Albert's first trip back in over seventy years—and Gorbachev personally had to approve his visit. Another of my mom's cousins was married to a woman whom I knew as Cousin Marjorie. She was a quiet, very lovely woman. Only a few years ago I found out she was actually the *Marjorie* that *Marjorie Morningstar* was written about.

The rest of the family was not quite as exotic. Hardworking people. The kind of people who spoke mostly Yiddish, which is a combination of German and phlegm. This is a language of coughing and spitting; until I was eleven, I wore a raincoat. These people love to eat and talk at the same time, so if you're on the other side of a sour cream conversation, they'll spray their breakfast all over you.

"No, no, no. He's a schmuck! He's a goniff! He's a putz. He's a prick!" If you're in a blue suit, you're a Jackson

Pollock like that! You end up wearing more than they ate.

My younger uncles were great guys. They were charismatic, great athletes, they drank a lot, had a lot of girlfriends. Picture the Kennedys, except they're eating flanken and playing mah-jongg. They were the Jewish Kennedys. I always thought the Kennedys would have been more fun if they were Jewish. It would have relaxed them a bit. Think of them around the table, during the holidays.

"Momma Rose, this lobster bisque is fantastic. What a novel way to break the Yom Kippur fast. Teddy, you're eating my kugel, Teddy. Stop eating my kugel, Teddy."

"Jack loves a shiksa. Jack loves a shiksa."

"You cut that out. Bobby, have a bissel of the tssimis, just a bissel."

"Some people see things the way

they are and say why, I dream things that never were and say, WHY THE HELL NOT?"

The older relatives weren't as much fun. They always looked miserable. They had faces like fists. Always with a frown. I called them the upside-down people, because if you put them upside down, they would look so happy. And they would argue about anything, like who was sicker.

"Murray, what are you talking about a fever. A hundred and six isn't a fever. I was in a coma for seven months. I never missed a day's work."

Cranky people but proud of their heritage. They were proud of who they were. There are some Jewish people today who are still uncomfortable being Jewish:

"Levine, party of six please."

"Excuse me. You mean Leviiine."

"Shapiro, party of four."

"Pardon me. You mean Shapiiiiro."

"FleCHman, are the FleCHmans here?"

"Excuse me. You mean Miller."

I have a theory as to why they were so miserable. I think they were miserable because they were hot. Let me explain: Open your family photo albums. Let's face it, we all have the same five relatives. They just jump from album to album.

They all looked exactly alike, and they all wore the same thing: big mink hats, beaver hats, earmuffs, gloves, mukluks, Persian lamb coats, mink coats, beaver coats . . . all at the same time. The women are wearing a fox stole, head, claws and tail, with a clasp that was always the fox biting its own foot. Wasn't that terrifying? It had a look in its glass eye that seemed to say, "How the hell did I end up here?" They were wearing stuffed animals, the Norman Bates line of clothing. It's like the old joke—two minks in the slaughter-house. One turns to the other and says, "Well, see you in shul."

I guarantee you, we all have this same photograph. A couple is standing there, covered with every conceivable pelt, hats pulled down over their ears, you can see just a sliver of their un-happy faces, and the caption reads: "At the beach, August, 1912." They're hot.

When I was growing up, we had this whole other group that was living with us. An extended family. This group was not speaking Yiddish. They were speaking a language that they actually made up themselves. This group was speaking jive talk. They were speaking hip talk. They were smoking cigarettes with no writing on them. They were jazz musicians, mostly African-American and some of the greatest players in the world. It was Jews and jazz forever. The house always smelled of brisket and bourbon. How did this happen? One man was responsible, and he unknowingly changed my life. It was my Uncle Milt Gabler.

Mom and Uncle Milt,
Silver Beach, 1932

Uncle Milt at the Commodore
Music Shop

CHAPTER 3

*F*or years and years, my grandfather had this little music store on 42nd Street between Lexington and Third that he called the Commodore Music Shop. And in it, he sold radios, electronic devices, that kind of thing. But during the summer months, he rented this little cottage on the ocean, a place called Silver Beach in Whitestone, under where the Throggs Neck Bridge is now. And at the end of the point, there was a wealthy man who had an estate. In the garden he had an outdoor dance pavil-

41

ion, which overlooked the sea, and he would hire Dixieland bands to play so his friends could dance and have an illegal cocktail.

During the summer months, my young Uncle Milt and his sister Helen, who would become my mom, would swim out to the point at night and hide by the dock treading water, watching the rich people party. Under those summer moons, my mom fell in love with dancing, and my Uncle Milt fell in love with the music, with the hot jazz.

Milt was a student at Stuyvesant High School in Manhattan, and after school he worked in my grandfather's store. So one day, with the music in his mind, he takes one of the speakers from one of the radios, puts it over the front door transom of the Commodore Music Shop and dials it into the local jazz station that plays Bix Beiderbecke records. Now the great Bix's hot cornet jazz is blasting out onto 42nd Street. And as people are walking by, hearing the music, they start changing direction, and coming into the store. "Hey, you guys sell these records?" But there weren't any.

So Milt gets an idea. He runs to his father.

"Hey, Pop."

"Don't sneak up on me, Milt. I thought you were a Cossack. I could have killed you."

"Pop, listen. We can sell jazz records. Everybody's coming in and wanting these jazz records, Pop. We should sell jazz records."

"Milt, why do I want to get involved with that crap for?"

"We could make a couple of bucks."

"Okay. I'm in."

*   *   *

So they start licensing the master recordings of out-of-print records from some of the local record companies in town, and they start reissuing these out-of-print records with just a plain, white label that said "Commodore" on them. And these reissued jazz records started selling really well.

Now young Milt starts going to all of the jazz clubs that were in Manhattan at the time. This is a particularly great time for jazz in New York. The clubs were all over town. In the Village, there was a club called Nick's. Then later, Eddie Condon, the great guitarist, opened his own club, and oddly enough he called it "Eddie Condon's." Jimmy Ryan's was on 52nd Street. And then there was Leon & Eddie's and the Onyx Club.

Milt starts going to Harlem and meeting all the great musicians in town from New Orleans, Kansas City and Chicago, all of these great original jazz giants, who play the same music but with different styles. And he gets another idea. He goes back to his father.

"Hey, Pop."

"Again with the sneaking up on me. Who died and made you a Cherokee? What is it?"

"Pop, listen. I want to produce my own records. Why are we making money for everybody else with these reissues for? I want to make my own jazz records, Pop. I can do it."

"Why would I want to get involved with that crap for? I hate jazz."

"We can make a couple of bucks."

"Okay. I'm in!"

So, on the day after Benny Goodman's legendary "Sing Sing Sing" concert in 1938—with Benny's searing clarinet and Gene Krupa's astounding, pulsating drum solo, Swing music was played for the first time ever in Carnegie Hall and it

45

knocked the music world on its ass—
Milt gets Goodman's sidemen and his
now good friends, the great jazz guitarist
Eddie Condon, and the best clarinetist in
town (Benny left town that morning),
Pee Wee Russell, and they go into a studio, and they do something my Uncle
Milt never did before in his life. He pro-
duces two records: "Jada" and "Love Is
Just Around the Corner." And the Commodore jazz label is born, the first inde-
pendently owned jazz label in the
world, and the records do great. Then
Milt gets yet another idea. He decides to
sell the discs by mail, so he starts something called "The United Hot Record
Club of America." He invented the mail
order business in the record industry.
He was only twenty-seven years old.

The word gets out to all the jazz
artists around the country, that there's
this young producer who has a great set
of ears and an even bigger heart. Now

everybody wants to do a session with my Uncle Milt on what is now our family business, the Commodore jazz label. Milt was a natural producer. He was a charismatic man, with a great laugh, and booming voice. He also was a great judge of character. He understood the musicians. He spent so much time getting to know them, he realized that he didn't have to get too creative with their talents. Make them comfortable, he thought, and make it sound like they were on stage "jammin'." He placed the microphones in the studio, so they would play together not separately, as was the norm, and he would simply bring a couple of bottles of whiskey, a carton of cigarettes, and turn them loose. He let them play it the way they felt it. He let them play it the way they created it. Sometimes, on one Commodore record, there would be three cuts of the very same song. He would

47

press all three cuts because there was a better solo, the beat was different, or there was just something about it that the musicians liked. He put them all on the same record, and they were grateful to him for it. He said, "Listen. Who am I to tell them how to play this? After all, this is jazz, America's only true art form."

So when I was a kid growing up, my father was now managing the Commodore Music Shop and he had become the authority on jazz and jazz records in the city. And this little store—it was only nine feet wide—was now the center of jazz not only in New York City but in the world, because that little mail order business was now third worldwide behind Sears Roebuck and Montgomery Ward, just selling Commodore and other jazz records.

Milt turned over the store and the running of the label to my father, his brother-in-law, because he went on to

become a vice president in charge of
Artists and Repertoire at Decca Records.
For thirty years, he had one of the greatest careers that any producer's ever had.
From 1941 to '73, he changed the way
that people listened to music, and not
just in jazz. In rhythm and blues, it was
the great Louis Jordan. Remember the
musical *Five Guys Named Moe*? That
was all of the music that they did together. And the big song that he co-
wrote was called, "Choo Choo Cha
Boogie," which actually brought about
the beginnings of rock and roll. In folk
music, it was the Weavers and Burl Ives.

In pop music, it was the Tommy
Dorsey Band, the Mills Brothers, the Ink
Spots, the Andrews Sisters, Bing Crosby,
Hoagy Carmichael, Judy Garland, even
Jerry Lewis's "Rock-a-Bye Your Baby." In
jazz, it was Louis Armstrong and Ella
Fitzgerald singing duets, and Lionel
Hampton. He also wrote "Danke

49

Schoen" for Wayne Newton and he told him, "Wayne, strap 'em up. You'll hit the high notes." The other songs he's responsible for: "Three Coins in the Fountain," "Volare," "Red Roses for a Blue Lady." In his career at Decca he produced thirty records that sold a million copies each. He's in the Grammy Hall of Fame, and the Rock and Roll Hall of Fame for a little thing he produced called "Rock Around the Clock" with Bill Haley and the Comets. "Rock Around the Clock" is one of rock's anthems, and ironically led to the demise of the music that Milt so loved, hot Dixieland jazz.

Going to the Commodore Music Shop was the greatest fun because now it was my dad's place. I remember my first trip in. It was my fifth birthday, the first time he and I went into the City alone together. We drove in from Long Beach. And that was the first time I saw the skyline from a distance, and I thought I was going to the Emerald City. We drove into the Midtown Tunnel, Dad explaining to me that we were now actually underwater. The tunnel was built under the East River connecting Manhattan and Long Island. I was scared. Especially when drops of condensation would hit the windshield. I thought for sure it was leaking, and soon we would be engulfed in water, like the Egyptians in the Red Sea. (I had seen *The Ten Commandments*.) Manhattan was incredible to me. The awesome buildings, towering over us. After we parked the car, we walked to the store. Dad pointed out the Chrysler Building, its silver skin gleaming in the morning sun. We went into this little coffee shop, and that's when I discovered my dad's secret life. As we sat down, the guy behind the counter came over, a big smile on his face.

"Hey, Jack. How you doing?"

"Good, Sam. How are you?"

51

"Who the hell is this guy?" I thought. "How does he know my father?" Now he smiled at me . . .

"You must be Billy, huh? I hear you're the funny one."

Who the hell is this guy?

"What are you going to have, Jack, the usual?"

"Yeah," Dad said. I couldn't believe it: My father had a usual! (I didn't know what a "usual" was, but it sounded important, so I wanted one.)

"So what are you going to have, Billy?" the counterman asked me.

"Um, the usual." So there I was having "the usual" with my dad—buttered roll, cup of coffee and a cigarette. I was five.

When you went to the store, you never knew who was going to be there. You'd walk in and Louis Armstrong would be there or Count Basie or Duke Ellington. Rosemary Clooney was in the store all the time. These were some of the people I was around when we were growing up. And the jazz was blasting through the speakers of the store. My grandfather was now basking in his new success, dealing with the patrons in his inimitable shy way.

"Hey. No dogs allowed in the store. What? I don't care if you're blind! Read the goddamn sign."

There were booths, so you could listen to the records and decide if you wanted to buy them or not. Everybody was listening or talking jazz. *Cosmopolitan* and *Life* magazine did pieces on the store and they called it "The Crummiest Shrine in the World."

That day, my fifth birthday, Dad gave me a broom and let me sweep the floor with him before the first customer came in. I loved doing that with him. He took me into one of the soundproof booths,

53

sat me down and put on the recording of *Peter and the Wolf.* I listened and watched him through the glass as he waited on customers. Everyone looked so happy to see him. I was getting to know him, in a different way. He seemed important to them also.

Later Pop took me out to lunch, just the two of us for the very, very first time. We stepped out of the store and headed west on 42nd Street. We passed the Commodore Hotel, which is how the store got its name. We went into Grand Central Terminal, past the Oyster Bar, up the ramp into the Great Hall with all of those people waiting. And I'm thinking, Why is he bringing me here on my birthday? And he said, "Bill, look at the ceiling. I come here every day for lunch. Isn't it magnificent? Happy Birthday kid."

It's so beautiful . . . a hand-painted map of the Zodiac, constellations, and all the heavens. It's still the best birthday I

ever had in my life, just sitting there
alone with my dad, having a Nedick's
hot dog under a beautiful sky of fake
stars.

That birthday was on a Friday, which
meant after the store closed, I got a special treat. I got to go to Dad's second
job. For seven years he had been producing free jazz concerts at a place
called Jimmy Ryan's on 52nd Street.
People loved the Sunday concerts at
3:00 in the afternoon. He never charged
admission, he did it for free just so people would get to know the music and
get to know these great musicians.
That's really all he cared about—the
music and these great players.

Dad put on concerts wherever he
could, Rye Playland, an amusement park,
on aircraft carriers for the Navy, even
Carnegie Hall, where he produced a
concert with the father of the blues,
W. C. Handy, who had written "St. Louis

Blues." Handy was blind, the first blind person I ever saw in my life. Dad had a special feeling for him, and so he started producing concerts at a place called the Lighthouse for the Blind in New York City, a wonderful center for sightless people. It was one of his favorite places to put on shows. I once asked him, "Why do you like it there so much, they can't see?" He said, "Yeah, but they hear better than anybody."

In 1949, he wanted a bigger venue so more people could hear the music, so he rented out a catering hall, a ballroom where they did weddings and bar mitzvahs, on the Lower East Side at 111 Second Avenue between 6th and 7th Streets. It was called the Central Plaza. And he started something there on Friday and Saturday nights that became sort of legendary in New York's jazz circles, and he simply called them "The Sessions."

Everybody came to play. With the rise of swing, and the modern jazz of Miles, Monk, Dizzy and Coltrane, the Central Plaza was one of the only places that these original Dixieland artists could come and jam, and the crowds would not only listen, but get up and dance. This is before rock and roll, so Dixieland jazz was the music that college kids would come into New York to dance to. The shows started at 7:00, and ended around 3:00 in the morning, usually when the great trumpet player Jimmy McPartland would stand up and play "When the Saints Go Marching In."

My dad was happiest there, I know it, because he got to produce these shows the way he wanted to. He didn't just book existing bands, he would put them together. The guys would call in looking for a gig, and every weekend he experimented with the players, like a chemist, always looking for the perfect

57

combination and the perfect sound. I used to love to answer the phone, not only because I thought someday somebody would call telling me they were going to take me to Hollywood, but I loved talking to the musicians. One of my favorites was Willie "The Lion" Smith. Willie was a very rare and charming man. He was a black Jewish man, who had also been a cantor in a synagogue at one time. He would call, and if I answered he would speak fluent Yiddish to me. I didn't know any Yiddish, but I would nod, and say "Hmm" once in a while, just so Willie would think I was following the conversation. I'd say, "Do you want to talk to my dad?" Willie would say, "Vat Den Bubbeleh, I like talking vit you, but you don't have any pockets." (Meaning Dad was the one who could pay him.)

A couple of years ago, *The New York Times* was doing a story on my dad, and

they asked me to talk to some of the sur-
viving musicians. One of Dad's regulars,
Conrad Janis, who is still a great trombone player, told me that Dad was the
"Branch Rickey" of jazz. And when I
heard that, I felt so proud because it
never occurred to me back then when I
was growing up.

It meant my dad was one of the first
producers to integrate bands, to play
black players with white players. And
oddly, that wasn't happening a lot even
in New York back in the late forties and
fifties, when the Central Plaza was at its
height. The players loved Dad because
he would do this, and he loved them
back. When he played them, he paid
them the best he could, and when they
died, he ran benefits for their families.
They really were his other set of sons,
and my brothers and I understood it, because we loved them too. If Dad made a
buck, he gave them eighty-five cents.

Which is probably why we had a gray-on-gray Plymouth Belvedere.

That night at the Plaza, I discovered my dad's other secret life. We were waiting for the show to start and he says to me, "Billy, don't you move. Don't move. I've got to do something. I'll be right back, and then we'll go downstairs to Ratner's and have cake. Don't move."

What he had to do was emcee the show. I didn't know that he did this too. Suddenly, there he was, behind the microphone. He had the audience in the palm of his hand. He was really charming and witty, and you could see how much he loved presenting this music to the world, and how much the players loved that he was the guy doing it. It was a thrill for me to see my dad behind that microphone. When I used to host the Grammy Awards, I would think that somehow I was channeling him, because I was doing the same thing he did decades before but I was introducing the great musicians of my day.

It was on this night, my fifth birthday, that I performed for an audience for the very first time. I was in the band room before the show with all of these fantastic musicians, a few I knew from the house, guys my uncle described as having "such big souls" and great names too: Hot Lips Page, Pee Wee Russell, Willie "The Lion" Smith, Buster Bailey, Henry "Red" Allen and the great Roy Eldridge.

Roy was a fantastic trumpet player and he wasn't very tall, so his nickname was "Little Jazz." When he met me for the first time, he called me "Littlest Jazz." Everybody else called me "Face." That was my nickname given to me by Zutty Singleton and Willie "The Lion" Smith. They were, along with Tyree Glenn, my favorites. They called me Face because I

61

could make their faces. I could imitate them and it was easy, because they were all such great characters. So, that night, somebody put me up on a sax case and that meant I had a stage.

"Hey, listen up, you got to hear what the Face can do. Face, do the joke about Zutty. Zutty, get over here. This is about you. Hit it, Face."

I imitated his voice and his mannerisms, eyes wide open, filled with joy, the voice, Satchmo-like, raspy from the cigarettes and the booze, a real nightclub voice, coming out of my five-year-old mouth . . .

"Zutty goes in to get his hair cut. He says to the haircut cat, 'How much is a haircut?'

"He says, 'Well, you know, a haircut is two dollars.'

"He says, 'Wow, two dollars. That's a little heavy for a haircut. How much is a shave?'

"'Well, you know, Zutty, a shave is just a dollar.'

"And Zutty said . . ." as I pointed to my hair, "'Okay, baby. Shave it.'"

Everyone cracked up. All of them coming over to give me some skin.

"Face, My Man the Face . . . Can you dig that? I knew that you could."

Then they ran up onstage and played. I was in heaven. The music went right into my soul. I was only five years old, but I understood my uncle and my dad just like that. I just fell in love with Dixieland jazz. For me it's easy because I think it's the happiest music in the world. And when it's good and it's really cooking, to me, Dixieland is like the end of the Kentucky Derby . . .

"And down the stretch they come. The trombone sets the pace, cornet takes the lead, clarinet comes up on the outside. Then the drummer goes to the whip, and it's a photo finish as they all cross the line together."

And I couldn't help myself. I ran up onstage and I started tap-dancing with them. Mom had been teaching me to tap-dance, but I only could get the right leg to work. The left just stood there watching the right one, as I danced to "Muskrat Ramble" spinning around only using my right leg, looking like a dog chasing its tail. The guys on the bandstand looked over and smiled, like I did this all the time, and the audience went wild. I loved every second. I think of that feeling every time I'm onstage. It's like my dad said, "Once you hear the music, you can't stand still."

Of all the great people who were recording for my uncle and being produced in concert by my dad, Billie Holiday was by far the greatest. I think there's only two artists, Sinatra and Billie, that when you hear one note, you know you're in the presence of a genius.

And I was so blessed to be in her presence when I was a little boy because of her relationship with my uncle and my dad. She used to call me Mister Billy and I would call her Miss Billie. She had done most of her great recordings on Commodore, and later followed Milt to Decca with songs like "Embraceable You," "Fine and Mellow," which he wrote with her, "Sunny Side of the Street," "As Time Goes By," "I Cover the Waterfront," "Good Morning Heartache" and "Lover Man."

But her most important song was one called "Strange Fruit," which was very controversial because it was about lynching black people down South. Nobody wanted to hear this song. When Billie introduced the song at the Café Society, nobody wanted to be reminded about what was happening in our Amer-

65

ica of 1939, and nobody would record "Strange Fruit." Even her great producer at Columbia Records, John Hammond, wouldn't touch it. She was frustrated, so she turned to her friend, my Uncle Milt. And he told me years later she sang it for him the first time a cappella. Can you imagine that? That aching voice and that aching lyric. "Southern trees bear a strange fruit, blood on the leaves and blood at the root, black bodies swinging in the Southern breeze. Strange fruit hanging from the poplar trees . . ." He told me, "Billy, I cried like a baby. And I said to her, 'Lady Day, listen, I don't care if we sell one record. People must hear this song. They've got to hear this song. We've got to get this made somehow.'"

So they worked out a special arrangement with Vocalian Records, and Billie Holiday, a great black jazz artist, and my Jewish Uncle Milt together recorded "Strange Fruit" a song about lynching down South, the song that *Time* magazine in December of 1999 would call the song of the century. I'm so proud to say it's on the family label, the Commodore.

One night, my dad was producing one of Billie Holiday's concerts. It was at a place called the Stuyvesant Casino, Second Avenue around 9th Street. We all got there in the afternoon to watch her rehearse and to hang out with Dad of course, and Miss Billie said something to me that totally changed my life.

"Hey, Mister Billy, let's go to the movies."

So Billie Holiday and I walked down Second Avenue together, past Ratner's, past the Central Plaza, to a little movie theater next door, called perfectly enough, the Loews Commodore. It later became known as the Fillmore East. And there sitting on Billie Holiday's lap, I saw my first movie. And the movie was

Shane: Alan Ladd, Van Heflin, Jean Arthur and JACK PALANCE! and this kid who I looked like, Brandon De Wilde. He was an extraordinary eight-year-old actor. I couldn't believe it. It proved to me that even if you're four foot six, you could be forty feet tall.

At the end of the movie, Shane rides off into the sunset. The kid runs after him and he screams, "Shane . . . come back."

And Miss Billie whispered in my ear, "He ain't never coming back."

I sat there, the projection light flickering behind me, the music swelling as well as the tears in my eyes, and I looked at that kid on the big screen, and I wanted it to be me. And you know something? It was a Sunday.

Aunt Sheila

CHAPTER 4

$\mathcal{M}$y grandmother once asked Louis Armstrong at a Seder, "Louis, have you tried just coughing it up?"

Louis laughed so hard, throwing his head back, pounding the table . . .

Grandma Susie was hilarious. She was my mom's mother, a big woman weighing around three hundred pounds. (At one time she was worth three electoral votes.) She was the One-Liner Queen. She had a great sense of humor. It made me think funny just being around her, and she could deal with any situation. One time, I walked in on her and she was naked. I mean, I loved her, but no one should ever have to see that. And she handled it better than I did.

"Oh, I bet you never thought you'd see this!" And she laughed and shut the door.

Me? Three years in therapy.

Her husband, my Grandpa Julius, was different. Julius was one of the hot people. He was one of the cranky people, and I think he was edgy because he was a little hard of hearing. He was always buying these new hearing aids from his connections with the store. Once a week he would try out a new hearing aid. The reason he tried out so many was every time he'd put a new one in, my brothers and I would do this to him:

"So, Gran—a how's —e ne- hear— -d? - -ope it -orks. Be—-se it -ooks -eally -ood. -'s nice and —all."

"What?"

"Is it —anese? -ow come —e Jap—ese -ake them so —all? Is— -ecause th-Japan— ar- so -s-m -all?"

"What?"

"Re—-ber — old on- —had -o —ear in —our —ocke-? Testing -, 2, -."

He'd pull the hearing aid out of his ear, and throw it across the room.

"God damn it. Another piece of shit. This is costing me a fortune."

I used to love when he would come over to stay with us. This was not a big house. The walls were paper-thin in this house. Oh, I never needed an alarm clock. I was never late for school. Six A.M. you'd hear him every morning, like a Jewish rooster, waking up the neighborhood. Coughing and hacking, wheezing, muttering to himself, "I can't get up the mucus." This was not just a cough, it was a plea for help.

Once he was done coughing, the farting would start. A true Whitman Sampler, every kind you can imagine, and some you can't possibly think could come from a human being. The problem was, he couldn't hear it. And when you're a little kid, that noise is the funniest thing you ever heard in your life, and he would keep talking, as he tooted away.

"Billy, you know what I think (fart) I'm going to do (fart). I want to go (fart, cough, fart) . . . I want to go (fart) . . . I want to go up on the board-walk. I want to go (fart) . . . I want to take a walk. Why are you walking so far behind me? Come, I want to be back around four because (fart) Grandma's making cabbage soup. I don't want to miss that. Phew!"

Then he would wave his hand

around like it was low tide, and of course, he would blame me: "Billy, what crawled up your ass and died? Do you feel all right?"

I used to love to have breakfast with him because that was like going to a science fair. He'd have a lot of plates on the table, he liked a lot of different tastes. He'd have a plate of just pieces of herring, a lot of herring, so for years, I thought he had a pet seal. There was a soup bowl of just soft-boiled eggs and a plate of toast, and then there was the ritual of the making of the glass of tea. This was something to watch. First, he would take the sugar cube, and put it between his teeth. Then he'd put his teeth in his mouth. He would then take the glass of tea, and he'd sip it through the sugar cube. When he was done, he'd walk over to the window, toot, toot, toot, take out the sugar cube and leave it on the windowsill to dry. He was eighty-nine when he died and he'd used two sugar cubes.

Breakfast with him was the greatest because we'd have these wonderful talks. I'd be sitting there, nine years old, waiting for him. He'd come down the hallway every morning in his grandpa uniform, his tank top and his boxer shorts with just a hint of his balls peeking out of the right side. Just enough to terrify you. I'd scream, "Joel! Grandpa's got an octopus in his shorts!" Some days, gravity would be a little stronger than other days, so from behind he looked like a Great Dane walking away.

"Billy, Billy (fart, fart, fart)." I couldn't help it, I started to giggle. "What's so funny? What are you laughing at? What, do you wake up laughing (fart, fart, fart)?" I was laughing so hard my ribs hurt. "Oy, I want your life.

"Billy, you're nine years old. What are you going to do with your life? You should know.

"When I was your age . . . I was nine years old. And I wasn't living in America. I was living in Austria in the village of (two coughs and a fart), and my parents wanted me to have a better goddamn future, so they put me on the boat alone at nine years old. The SS *Rotterdam*. I came to America. I landed at Ellis Island August third, 1903. On August the fourth, I got a job. Nine years old, I got myself a pushcart, and I would push it up the street. Which is how it got its name, pushcart. So I said to myself after a month of doing this, 'Schmuck, put something in it. You're pushing an empty cart!' That's why business was off. I didn't have a plan! So, I bought a piece of cloth for three cents, and I split it in half. I sold them both for ten and made a goddamn profit, kid. So, now I had a plan. I would buy cloth. I would split it, and I would sell it for a profit. And I would save my money, kid. Because, Billy, I had a plan.

"After a while, I bought my first store, a little dress shop, Fulton Street in Brooklyn, proudest day of my goddamn life. Then I wanted the store next to me so I could expand. So I worked harder. Every day, forty-eight hours a day, saving my money. I ate wood. I drank sand. And I bought the store next to me, knocked the wall down, now it was bigger yet. Then I bought the next store, bigger yet, bigger yet. I had the whole goddamn block. Saved my money because I had a plan, kid. I reached back across the Atlantic, got my family, and we were reunited here in America. Then I turned ten."

I believed every word. Here was a self-made kid. Heroes don't have to be public figures of any kind. Heroes are right in your family. There's amazing stories in all of our families, you just have to ask, "And then what happened?"

And heroes don't have to look like Derek Jeter. They can also have way too much makeup on and cotton candy hair, like my Aunt Sheila. She's heroic to me because she's a tough lady. Some people say she's got a big mouth, and she does, but I admire that about her, because she speaks the truth, and sometimes people don't like to hear the truth, especially in families.

She lives in Boca Raton, Florida. What a shock! It's a perfect place for her to live because in Spanish, Boca Raton means "mouth of the rat." She's been down there for years, and never once has she had a tan, because she's always inside, talking on the phone.

Recently, she went through something that was very tough to get through, and she came through it with flying colors . . .

"Hello. Hello, Reba. How are you, dear? I got your message, we were at the movies, we went to see *The Passion of* . . . you know who. Can I tell you something, I was outraged . . . No, the movie was fine. Popcorn was seven dollars! Leonard said, 'Watch . . . this they'll blame on us too.' Hold on just for a second.

"Leonard, get the car . . . Leonard, get the car . . . Get the goddamn car . . . Just pull it up, please. I'm tired . . .

"Hello? . . . No. He and I are in the middle of a thing . . . Because he lied to me . . . He bought something off one of those fakakta TV ads . . . He bought a videotape for nineteen dollars and he kept it from me. He didn't want me to see it, but I found it when I was looking for loose change. It's the one with the college girls that come down here on spring break and show their knockers . . . So I didn't know that he had it. He would disappear into the TV room with this knocker tape, close the door, and for hours at a— hold on just a second . . . LEONARD! Maybe it's not tennis elbow!

"So, Reba, I stormed in there. I said, nineteen dollars for knockers? Nineteen dollars for knockers? So, I hiked up my blouse and let them out. 'Look, these you can have for free!' He said, 'No, thank you,' and ordered Volume 2.

"LEONARD! Get the goddamn car, please . . . Pull it up . . . You're on my list, mister.

"Hello . . . ? Hello? Reba . . . ? Reba, Reba . . . ? Hello? Hello . . . ? Oh, there you are. I was afraid I lost you. I walked over to a place in the hallway where the phone never works, right in front of a picture of Leonard's mother.

"Good. He's gone. Now listen. I'm going to tell you a story, Reba, but promise me that you won't be mad. Just promise me. Okay. Julie got married . . . You said you weren't going to be mad. Don't make a promise if you can't keep it. What is that . . . ? Look, I know she's your goddaughter, but she's my only daughter, so let me just tell you the goddamn story! Let me just tell you the goddamn story! And I promise you won't be mad. Okay?

"You know how she always had boyfriends but it never worked out because she was so picky? She always found something wrong with them. Remember . . . ?

"Okay. Five years ago she comes down here, and she says, 'Sit down . . .' So we do. 'I'm gay.' . . . No, not me.

Her. Is this how you follow the story . . . ? Yes, your goddaughter is gay. I was floored. So I said, 'Really? Are you sure? Maybe it's a phase. You know, maybe it's like the Macarena. It will come and it will go and nobody will care.'

"So she said to me, 'No, Ma. No. I think I've always been this way. Yeah, since I'm a little girl.' I said, 'What?' She said, 'Yeah. I just didn't know what it was.' She said, 'Mom, you know what? I'm out.' And I said, 'Of what, dear?' 'Out of lies, out of secrets,' she says. 'No more pressure, no more hiding. This is who I am. And I feel great about it, and I want it to be okay with you and Daddy . . .'

"What are you going to do? It's your daughter. She's in pain. So I said, 'Listen, darling. I don't care what you are. I love you even more now that you were able to tell us. You're my daughter, and I'll love you forever.'

"I thought I handled it great. Schmendrik didn't handle it well. No. Leonard gets upset when he hears the news. He doesn't say anything, and his face fills up with blood. You know, his eyes bulge out of his head, his face gets all red, he looks like a cherry tomato . . . Cherry tomato? The little hard ones . . . Remember that salad bar in Aventura we used to go to, they had those little cherry tomatoes that would explode in your mouth, like some nasty little surprise . . . ? Or better yet, he looks like that baboon's tuchis at Parrot Jungle. Remember when we went there?

"And when I see his face look like that, there's only one thing I can say to him. 'Leonard, get the car.' And we took a drive up and down Alligator Alley just talking and talking. All the time he kept saying to me, 'Sheila, how could she do this to me? How could she do this to me?'

"I said, 'Leonard, she didn't do anything to you. Don't make this about you. Why are you making this about you?'

"He said, 'You don't understand. When Julie was a little girl, we used to play wedding together. And I would say to her, Julie, at your wedding, you and I are going to dance the first dance together to "Sunrise, Sunset" and now— Yeah . . . From *Fiddler*. Is there another one . . . ? No, Reba. 'Sunrise, Sunset' from *The Wiz* . . .

"He said, 'Now it's not going to happen. She's our only daughter, and now she's a gay person, and I don't even want to talk to her.'

"I said, 'Listen to yourself, don't you ever say that.' I was so mad, but inside, Reba, I was very concerned too. Because let's face it. She is our only daughter, and Leonard and I are the only barren grandparents in our cul-de-sac.

"It was very tense between the two of them for years and years and years after that . . . Reba, I'm telling you now.

"Last month, Julie calls from San Francisco. She said, 'Folks, sit down. I've got to tell you something.'

"'Okay. What is it now?' I said to myself.

"She said, 'I'm getting married.'

"I said, 'To a wo— who?'

"'Olivia,' she tells me.

"I said, 'Olivia? I thought she was your housekeeper . . .' Because every time I'd call, Olivia would answer. I figured if you're calling and a woman's there, she's cleaning.

"And she says, 'No. She's my partner . . .' That's what they call them,

86

Reba. They call them 'partners.' No, no, no. Tonto was a faithful companion.

"She says, 'You've got to come. It's on Valentine's Day. It won't be the same if you and Dad are not there.'

"I said, 'Of course we'll be there. Daddy and I will be there. Give my love to Olivia. We love you both.'

"I thought I handled it great. Schmendrik didn't handle it well. No. Leonard gets all upset. He starts with the yelling . . . 'I'm not going.'

"I said, 'You're going.'

"He said, 'I'm not going.'

"I said, 'You're going!'

"'I'm not going.'

"I said, 'You're going.' So I made him a Judy Garland, nine Seconals, half a quart of Vodka, stuffed him in the pet carrier and loaded him on the plane.

"So we get to San Francisco. I've never been there before. It's beautiful there. But you know something? There are a lot of gay people there. I mean, a lot. It's like Starbucks, they're on every corner.

"So we go to the City Hall there. They're being married by a justice of the peace . . . No. A man . . . And all of their friends are there. Lovely women I have to say. Lovely women. Olivia teaches third grade . . . Of course they let her. It's not contagious, Reba.

"Then, during the service, they say these vows, which they wrote to each other. Reba, they were so beautiful. How they met, when they fell in love, what they want for the rest of their lives. They were so loving. I couldn't believe it. It was—it was wonderful. I had a tear in my eye. But then at the end of the service they— No. No, darling. They don't step on a glass and scream 'l'chaim,' no. This is not a Jewish service. This is a lesbiterian service . . . But then at the very, very end of the service, they kissed. I mean a real boy-and-girl kiss.

"So after I came to, we go to the reception. Olivia's parents throw the reception, at a beautiful ranch that they own out in a place called Napa. Her father does very well. He's got a lot of money. He makes knockoffs of costume jewelry. All of their friends made all the food . . . No caterer. They made the food themselves. Let me tell you something, Reba. Best food I've had at any affair. You may not agree with their lifestyle, Reba, but these lesbians can cook. I had a short rib on a bed of Condoleezza Rice that was so delicious . . . the meat fell away from the bone. It was— Why? What did I say? What did I say? I said basmati rice . . . I didn't . . . ? I said Condoleezza . . . ? I said Condoleezza . . . ? Well, she's been on my mind.

"But then the head of the trio made

this announcement to everybody at the reception: 'Ladies and gentlemen, please welcome to the dance floor for the very, very first time as a married couple, Julie and Olivia.' Okay. Guess what they dance to . . . ? 'Sunrise, Sunset'! I plotzed. I couldn't believe it, Reba. There's my daughter dancing with her wus-band to that song. I looked at Leonard and that baboon tuchis face is filling up with blood, his eyes are bulging out of his head. He's so mad he stands up and he walks right out . . . onto the dance floor. He came up behind Julie. She didn't see him coming. He taps her on the shoulder. She turned around, saw that face and said, 'What is it, Daddy?' And he said to her, 'May I have this dance?' And he bowed . . .

"No, I'm here, I'm getting emotional . . . They start dancing. First a box step. Then another box step. Then

90

he starts whirling her around and twirling her around. Because you know Leonard. He's fat, but he's so light on his feet. Oh Reba, the sight of them dancing and smiling after all of those hard years . . . I tell you, Reba, I just—I got reminded about how much I love this fat, little bald guy who tips eleven percent. So I got up and I danced with Olivia! . . . You bet your ass I did. And then I danced with her mother too. And then her father danced with Leonard! And before you know it, we were all in a lesbian hora.

"Reba, the sight of Leonard dancing with all of those lesbians . . . if there was a tape of him for nineteen dollars, I would have bought it. You know something? It was the greatest wedding I've ever been to in my life. I'm telling you, we're on cloud twelve, you can see nine from there. You know, it's just unbelievable. We're just so happy . . .

"What do you mean does it count? Of course it counts. It was in the City Hall by a justice of the peace. It's official. She said, 'I love you,' she said 'I love you.' They kissed and we had cake. To me, that's a wedding . . .

"Reba, you can't tell me my daughter's wedding wasn't a wedding, you didn't hear the vows. They love each other, the same way you love your Herbie . . . You can't tell me that's not a wedding . . . Hello . . . ? Hello . . . ? Reba, I'm losing you . . . I'm losing you. Reba?"

She turns to see she's standing in front of the picture of Leonard's mother . . .

"IT'S A FUCKING WEDDING YOU SAD SACK OF SHIT! AND IT FUCKING COUNTS!

"Hello . . . ? Oh, there you are. I was

afraid I lost you . . . No. I was just saying how happy we are for them. But listen, there's more. Congratulate me and I'll tell you why . . . Just congratulate me and I'll tell you why because I'm bursting with the news . . . We are going to be grandparents! . . . Yeah. They called today. They adopted a baby together. A girl . . .

"What? No it's not a lesbian, she's eight days old! Give her time. What the hell's the matter with you? Don't step on my happiness. They're getting her next week, isn't that something? A little brown-skinned, black-haired Cambodian baby named Tiffany . . .

"Reba, you're crying . . . Reba, why are you crying? Tell me . . . Oh, that's so sweet. Now we won't be the only barren grandparents in our cul-de-sac . . . No. I love you, too . . . You know I do . . . I love you. You love me. Far Rockaway High School forever . . .

Now you got me crying too. Reba, you know what it is? Maybe it's not what you dreamt about. It's not what you thought would ever happen when they first hand them to you after they're born. You know?

"Sometimes things work out different than you want for your kids. But you know what . . . ? It is what I wanted, because she's happy. That's it, and that's all, as long as they're happy, and they're *so* happy, I mean, who's hurting who here? Who's hurting who?

"Okay. Listen, we're going out to dinner to celebrate the baby. Do you want to come . . . ? I know it's two in the afternoon but it's dinnertime. It's Boca . . .

"Oh, you already ate? . . . Reba you're not mad, are you . . . ? Told you . . . Goodbye.

"Hey, Grandpa? Get the goddamn car!"

Me at age five

Me and
Mickey Mantle

CHAPTER 5

*M*ay 30, 1956. Dad takes us to our first game at Yankee Stadium.

We were in Nellie driving under the elevated subway of Jerome Avenue, and the sun was playing peek-a-boo with the railroad tracks. We pulled into the parking lot. We got out and I said, "Where's the field, Pop?"

He pointed to the stadium. "There."

I said, "In that building?"

He said, "Yeah. Come on, guys. Let's go. Hurry up. Come on. Let's go."

I held on to the back of Dad's sport jacket, and we ran to the stadium with my brothers behind me. And as we got closer to the stadium, we got more excited. "Tickets, please. Yearbooks here. Programs. Tickets, please. Hey, there you go, sir."

The ticket taker rubbed my head: "Enjoy the game, little man."

I'm in the concourse of the stadium now. Men in white shirts and ties on their way to a hot Memorial Day doubleheader. I'm eight years old, and I grab on to Pop's hand, as we walk through one of those passageways toward the field. It was so dark, you couldn't see anything, but you could smell it. The smell of hot dogs and beer, mustard, relish, and pickles embedded in the concrete ever since the days that the great Babe Ruth had played there.

And then suddenly, we were there.

The enormous stadium, the blue sky with billowing clouds that God hung like paintings looming over its triple decks, which in turn hovered over an emerald ocean. The people in the bleachers, seemingly miles away, would be watching the same game we would be. The three monuments sitting out there in deep center field, three granite slabs with brass plaques on them for Lou Gehrig, Miller Huggins and The Babe, and I thought they were actually buried in the outfield. The players in the classic pinstripe uniform, the interlocking NY over their hearts, running, throwing, laughing with each other, as if they were knights on a mystical field.

Dad took out his eight-millimeter camera to take movies so that we would never forget. But how could you? How green the grass was, the beautiful infield, the bases sitting out there like huge marshmallows, the

99

Washington Senators in their flannel uniforms warming up on one side, and the Yankees taking batting practice on the field. The first time I heard the crack of the bat. It was so glorious. We had a black and white TV, so this was the first game I ever saw in color. We had Louis Armstrong's seats that day, and before the game started, Louis had arranged for us to go to the Yankee Clubhouse. Joel had a slipped disc in his back, and Dad had been very worried about him, so Louis got the Yankee trainer, Gus Mauch, to examine Joel's back. We stood just outside the clubhouse, as Gus worked on Joel's back, and suddenly Casey Stengel walked out. I blurted out, "Who's pitching?" Casey didn't hesitate: "You are kid, suit up!" Someone took my program into the clubhouse, and it came out with several autographs on it, most notably Mickey Mantle's. I felt like I was holding the Holy Grail. They led us back to our seats, and I was sitting on my knees because I couldn't see over this rather large priest who was sitting in front of me in his black suit and white collar.

In the fourth inning, Mickey Mantle, Elvis in pinstripes, twenty-five years old, in his Triple Crown summer, batting left-handed, off Pedro Ramos, hit the longest home run without steroids in the history of Yankee Stadium. It went up through the clouds and struck off the facade of the once mighty copper roof. And as the ball ascended the heavens, the priest stood up blocking my vision of my first home run. And all I heard him say, in his Irish accent was, "Holy fucking shit!"

Later, Mickey hit a triple, and he rumbled into third base and pulled himself up like a runaway mustang. And there he was right in front of me, No. 7, in the afternoon sun. Then I knew who I wanted to be. I wanted to be Mickey Mantle. I was eight years old, but I walked like him, with a limp. My bar mitzvah I did with an Oklahoma drawl. "Shemaw Israw-el . . . Today I am a ballplayer." And that's all we did, Joel, Rip and I, was play baseball.

That's all I wanted to be . . . a Yankee. Then on Sundays, Dad would take us out to the Long Beach High School baseball field to teach me how to hit the curveball, which he had mastered. He was a pitcher at Boys High in Brooklyn, and played sandlot ball, and he still had a great curveball. And all summer I couldn't hit it. As the ball came toward me, I thought it was going to hit me, and I would bail out, and it would break over the plate.

"Bill, don't be scared up there. Wait on it. Watch it break, and hit it to right. Okay? Wait on it and hit it to right."

Those summer Sundays belonged to October now. The leaves had changed. We're in sweaters. World Series weather we used to call it, and I still couldn't hit his curveball. October became November. "Wait on it." November became December and we're still out there. It's hard to hit a curveball anyway, but curveballs in the snow?

"All right, kid. Come on, Billy. You can do this now." He blew on his hand to warm it, smoke coming out of his mouth.

He wound up, and as it whistled toward me, Dad whispered loudly, "Wait on it . . ." I watched it curving away through the falling flakes . . . CRACK! The ball sailed into right field and buried itself in the snow. I looked at it in wonder, my red nose running, my hands tingling with excitement. I

103

looked at Dad. He smiled. "Now you're getting it. Now you're getting it."

Rip retrieved it, and threw it to Joel, who tossed it to Dad. "Okay, let's do it again." He started his windup and threw me another beauty . . . "Wait on it." CRACK!

Baseball became a huge part of our lives. Joel, Rip and I would always head out to the mall in front of our house. It was a grassy island in the middle of Park Avenue, about seventy-five yards long, with some trees on it, traffic moving in both directions on either side of it. But to us, it was our stadium. We would always be out there, playing ball. Traffic would slow down to watch us. We'd practice double plays, play "running catch," which meant you had to throw it over someone's head so they would have to make a difficult play. Sometimes drivers would honk their horns in appreciation. We would fungo hard grounders at each other, and if you could field a grounder on that mall, you could field anywhere. We always played with a baseball. There was no organized Little League in Long Beach, and the schoolyard games were always on concrete, played with a softball. That's why those Sunday batting sessions with Dad were so important, because we were playing good old-fashioned hard ball.

I did everything I could to make myself a better player. To practice, I took a golf ball, and my glove, and I would go to our tiny backyard and throw it off the concrete wall of the garage so it came at me at great speeds. I'd catch it, and I'd throw to either side, harder and harder so my reflexes got to be really fast. Then I would move closer. It was like pulling a bullet out of the air. I could catch anything, and I learned not to be afraid of the ball.

When I started to play baseball in ninth grade for Long Beach High, no matter how hard a ball was hit to me, I had seen faster.

Imitating players also helped me develop skills. The Yankees had a second baseman named Bobby Richardson, who had great hands, and could get rid of the ball very quickly. I would study him, his feet, his posture, where he held his hands before the pitch, how he made the pivot on the double play, and just as I could imitate my grandfather, the musicians and other relatives, I would "do" Bobby Richardson. Eventually, like a good impersonation, you put yourself into it so it becomes a blend of the best of you and the best of the person you're imitating. And I became a really good-fielding second baseman and shortstop with my own style.

Just because your dad takes you out

and tries to teach you how to play baseball, doesn't mean you have to like it. I loved it, because he was so patient with us. He loved the simplicity and the beauty of baseball, and because of that we loved it too. I would go on to play and become the captain of our high school team. I also played basketball and soccer for Long Beach High, but baseball was really my sport. All those years playing with Joel and Rip were some of our best times. We weren't competing for laughs or attention, or having our occasional fights. Baseball was the great equalizer. All we had to do was throw the ball to each other and say, "Nice catch," or sometimes, nothing at all.

Joel was a graceful player, tall at six foot two, and lean. He played first base and the outfield, and was a strong power hitter. Rip was left handed, so he played outfield and pitched. Rip was a nickname; we're still not sure how he got it—Richard was his given name—but some claim it was because he loved this player named Rip Ripulski. Others say it was because he kept ripping his pants. Only two years older than I, Rip was a very charismatic kid. He was handsome, a talented musician and singer, great personality, girls loved him. His legacy at school was a tough one to live up to.

He had amazing energy, always walked ahead of us, sometimes by as much as a block, which drove Mom and Dad crazy when we were in Manhattan with its crowded streets. We shared the room in the back, and he could drive me nuts. Too much energy, even for sleep. He'd kick his leg, like a metronome, over and over into the mattress. He'd keep me up, and, I'd yell, "STOP WITH THE LEG," and he'd be fast asleep, still kicking. Today he'd be on a Ritalin drip. That's one of the few things we would ever fight about, kicking that damn leg.

Joel, six years older than I, was quieter than Rip, but who wasn't? Really fast and funny, he always had a great line for any situation. Joel also had a natural ability to draw. Sketching and painting came easy to him. When Mom and Dad would be out together, he would invent games for us to play. He took his first baseman's glove, a plastic golf ball, and Mom's three iron. He'd sit in a chair, in one corner of the living room, and Rip and I would take turns hitting the ball at him, as if we were hockey players, and Joel was the goalie. You would get ten shots "on goal," and then we would rotate. The one who saved the most shots was the winner. Our hallway became a bowling alley, complete with minature pins. He made a small basketball hoop, like those Nerf ones that are so popular now, which we would hook over his bedroom door, and with a tennis ball, his room became Madison Square Garden. The best game, and one that would become important to us, was "Bird."This was our version of stickball.

Our little backyard had the same physical layout as Yankee Stadium—short right field, which was where the garage was, and deep left center, which was the back wall of the house. There was a cement patio, which simulated an infield, and a small diamond-shaped patch of grass, ending in a dirt patch, our home plate.

Joel fashioned a strike zone out of some kind of drywall material, and attached it to a painting easel, and that stood at home plate. We used a badminton shuttlecock as a ball, and a Little League bat, and we played a "baseball" game back there, with our

own intricate set of rules. If the shuttlecock hit off this window it's a double, the higher window it's a home run,
et cetera.

And not only did we play, we also
"broadcast" the games. I was Red Barber or Mel Allen, two of the greatest
Yankee announcers, and we would call
the game as we played it. Houses were
on top of each other, so the neighborhood would hear the action. We would
pick teams. I was always the Yankees,
Joel was the St. Louis Cardinals, Rip
was the Dodgers. We had a pregame
and postgame show in the garage "studio." Neighbors would call Mom, saying, "I fell asleep, who won the game?"

There was a newsletter, and we
even played an "Old-Timers Game," imitating the former Yankee Greats, playing a few innings as old men. We
played night games by taking all the
lamps out of the living room, removing

111

the shades and with the use of a few extension cords, placing them around the backyard. We played doubleheaders and, of course, the World Series. Our home was a two-family house. There was a one-bedroom apartment upstairs, where Abe and Estelle Marks lived. They weren't happy with us.

After all, they lived over Yankee Stadium, Madison Square Garden, and a bowling alley. She was English, and during one of our more spirited "Bird" games, she yelled down to us from her bedroom window (the left field bleachers), "I know it's the World Series, but Abe just had surgery."

We played "Bird" until I moved to California. I was twenty-eight years old.

Remember that program Mantle signed in 1956? Well in 1977, I was on *Soap*, playing the first openly homosexual character in a network show, and ABC had me appear on every talk show. I called it the "I'm not really gay tour." Mickey was a guest on the Dinah Shore show, and I brought the program, and he signed it again, 21 years later. We became good friends, with Mickey sometimes telling me very intimate stories about his life, usually over too many drinks. I always wanted to pick up a phone and call Dad when I was with Mickey. When Mickey died, the night before the funeral, Bob Costas and I spent the night in a Dallas hotel, writing his eulogy, which Bob would so eloquently deliver.

In 1991, the Anti-Defamation League named me the entertainer of the year, and gave me an original seat from Yankee Stadium. It was given to me at the premiere of *City Slickers*. In the film I talk about my "best day" being that first game at the stadium. Mickey signed the seat for me. It reads: "Billy, wish you was still sitting here, and I was still playing." When Mickey died, I thought my childhood had finally come to an end.

Dad and Mom

CHAPTER 6

round 3:00 on a Sunday, Dad would take out his mandolin and he'd play. He'd sit in the living room, at the end of the couch, the afternoon sun would come streaming through the Venetian blinds, making him look like he was playing the mandolin in prison. We always gave him this time, even if it ate into our day. If it was an hour out of our Sunday, what difference did it make? He worked so hard all week. He deserved an hour to do what he wanted to do. So as soon as he picked

117

up the mandolin, everybody left him alone . . . except me. I would come down the hallway, and I would sit at the edge of the living room where he couldn't see me, just out of sight around this column, and I would watch him play the mandolin at three o'clock on a Sunday. I don't think he ever saw me, but I always like to think that he knew that I was there.

He was a fascinating man to me. He was a St. John's University Law School graduate, class of 1931, but he never practiced. He gave it up because he fell in love with two things: Dixieland jazz, and my mother.

They were so different. Dad was a very quiet man. He was very witty. Everybody loved him. He was a very charming guy, and kind. But as kind as he was, he also could be quick-tempered and he could look dour a little bit, sad sometimes. He had Duke Ellington eyes. My mom had a smile like Times Square. She could light up a room with her big personality. For all of her bravado, however, she was also very sentimental. She was a wonderful singer and dancer, a natural performer. I think she could have been a terrific actress. Together, they were both very athletic. Dad was good at anything, and Mom was a strong golfer, bowler, and a graceful swimmer.

They met at Macy's in 1935. They both worked there. Dad was in the legal department and my mom was in notions. She had this little notions counter where she sold stray thoughts, concepts and ideas. Mom was in the Macy's theater group, which did plays and musicals, and for a few years was the voice of Minnie Mouse in the Macy's Thanksgiving Day Parade. Those big forty-foot-high floats would come down Broadway, and Mom would sit inside the float with a microphone and sing Minnie Mouse's favorite song, "I'm Forever Blowing Bubbles," with thousands of people lining the boulevard.

They were very affectionate with each other. Always holding hands in front of us, a kiss on the cheek, arm around each other. It was always nice to feel that your parents were still in love.

When he was done with the mandolin, he'd put it down and pick up this book by Will Durant, *The Life of Greece*. He was fascinated by the Greeks. He thought they were the greatest civilization of all. Everything about the Greeks interested him—the mythology, the democracy, the plays, the tragedies, the comedies, Euripides, Socrates, Aeschylus, Plato. He knew the islands, Mykonos, Santorini, and Crete, like the palm of his hand. He talked about them like he had been there several times. So when it came time for us to take the one family trip that we would get to take together, there was really only one place for us to go . . . the Catskills.

We jumped in the Belvedere, made three left turns, and headed north. I grabbed the camera and started taking pictures of the countryside on our way to the legendary Catskills, the only mountain range in the world that if Osama bin Laden was hiding there, somebody would say to him, "Oh, so you're single!"

We got to Kutscher's. My first hotel. That huge pool . . . so much room for me to hang on to the side and pee. And they had this gigantic dining room. The energy was astounding, a thousand Jews fighting over end cuts. In that week there were things that totally changed my life. That's when I first rode a horse, becoming a real city slicker. I saw my parents taking mambo lessons in public, and I saw Wilt Chamberlain wearing the uniform of the Harlem Globetrotters. That's the team he played with the year before he came into the NBA. Wilt, a former bellboy at Kutscher's, was there playing with other pros in a basketball clinic.

But on Saturday nights in the Catskills, the comedian is the king. I had never seen a comic in person before. Holding on to my pop's hand, we walked into the Kutscher's nightclub, and that's when I saw my very first comedian. He was introduced, the combo played him on, and there he was, in a spotlight, doing a funny walk, cigarette in one hand, looking so confident, and almost regal.

"Good evening, ladies and Jews. What a night. Oh, I had a rough night. I came home and found my wife in bed with my best friend. So I said, 'Lenny, I have to, but you?'"

My first rim shot. The combo on-stage laughed, I saw them looking at each other. Somehow I thought that was cool. It was all so exciting.

"This guy goes to the doctor. He says, 'Doc I have five penises!' The doctor said, 'How do your pants fit?' He said, 'Like a glove!'"

Rim shot! Screams from the crowd. Mom and Dad looked a little uncomfortable, I was giggling like crazy because he said Penis on stage, Joel and Rip were going nuts.

"This little boy is playing with his testicles. He says, 'Mommy, are these my brains?' She says, 'Not yet!'"

I watched him prowl the stage like a panther in a sharkskin suit. His timing was unbelievable. He wore the audience down. The audience was six inches shorter when they left the show. And as I'm sitting there at nine years old, watching this comic, I have this

123

epiphany. I say to myself, I could never play baseball like Mickey Mantle ever, but this I could do. I memorized his act instantly.

The next weekend, all the relatives were coming over to the house. There could be thirty-five or forty of them sitting right there in the living room, which to me meant: Show time. I took the comic's act that I'd just seen, and I changed it just a little bit to suit my crowd.

"Well, good evening, family of Jews. Boy, Grandpa had a rough day. I mean, rough. He came home and found Grandma in bed with Uncle Mac. He said, 'Mac, I have to, what's new?' (I then made two fart noises and coughed three times. They roared.)

"Uncle Barney came over and said, 'I got a new pair of pants.' I said, 'How do they fit?' And he said, 'I don't know, I can't get them on, I have five penises.'"

The rim shot went off in my mind. I did a take and held it, just like the comic had. The room was alive to me, the relatives laughing.

"Grandpa went to the doctor. The doctor said, 'Julius, we'll need a sample of your urine, blood and stool.' He said, 'Fine. Take my underwear.'"

Pow! Huge laugh. I was out of jokes. "What a family. You've been a great family."

Oh, my God. Oh, my God. I ran to my room. The laughter went right into my soul. Oh, it felt so good. Destiny had come to me. I was only nine years old, but it's clear what I was going to be. I was going to be a comedian. There was no confusion. This is what I was going to do with my life. I had never been happier.

Until. I heard my parents in the next room in their bedroom through the paper-thin walls.

"Jack, you're going to have to talk to him. Five penises? What the hell was that?"

"Helen, he took the comic's act and he changed it."

"I know. But take my underwear, urine, blood and stool? That's my father."

"I know. Helen, he just did the comic's act, and he—"

"I know, but my mother is crying. Schtupp Uncle Mac? That's her brother-in-law! She doesn't even like Uncle Mac. That's my mother he's talking about."

"I know. I know."

"I mean, you have to talk to him."

"I will talk—"

"I want you to talk to—"

"I will talk—"

"I want you to talk—"

"I'm going to talk to him, but I'm not going to talk to him tonight, Helen.

He was so happy. Did you see how happy Billy was? I'll talk to him tomorrow."

I heard that whole thing. And it taught me a very important lesson. Live in a house with thicker walls. Who needed to hear this shit? I was funny.

The next day Dad took me aside. "Billy, Bill—" He stared at me for a few seconds, and then he burst out laughing. "You were really funny. But listen. You got to know your audience, kid. Know your audience."

"Pop, listen. I want to be a comedian. Is that crazy? I loved it. I just loved it. I want to be a comedian."

"Billy, it's not crazy because I think you can be one, and I'm going to help you."

The next day, Dad brought home something from the store that really started to change my life. He brought home a tape recorder. A Webcor reel-to-reel tape recorder. It was profound for us because then there was no videotape or anything like that. This was the only way we could hear ourselves back. We could make up our own TV shows and radio shows, practice our imitations. We would do our shows in the living room for the relatives, and hear them back. This was the way to develop our own timing.

Then Dad started taking the time to show us the really funny people on television to inspire us. He would let us stay up late on school nights, to watch Ernie Kovacs, the great Steve Allen with Tom Poston and Don Knotts and Louis Nye, and the greatest comedian ever to grace television, Sid Caesar. The first time I saw Sid's show, I remember they were doing the "This Is Your Life" sketch. And Sid, playing the man whose life was being honored, was having a tearful reunion with his "Uncle Goopy"

(Howard Morris). They would wrestle each other, crying and overcome with emotion. Every time Sid would leave the embrace, Uncle Goopy would leap at him, and mighty Sid would carry him around the room.

It was breathtakingly funny. Our whole family roared with laughter as we watched. That's how I went to sleep every night for months afterward. I was Uncle Goopy and Dad was Sid, and he would carry me, laughing hysterically, to bed. He'd put me in bed, only to have me leap on him and start all over again. Watching Sid with Carl Reiner, Imogene Coca, and Howard Morris made me want to be a comedian. I was just a little boy, but it was hilarious to me. No wonder, some of the writers were Larry Gelbart, Neil Simon, Mel Brooks, Woody Allen, and Carl Reiner.

Every Sunday night, Ed Sullivan would have a comedian on, and that comedian was always Alan King. There was *Bilko*, and *The Honeymooners*, Red Skelton, even a funny game show in the afternoon hosted by a hilarious young man named Johnny Carson.

Every day after school, I would watch Laurel and Hardy, hosted by Chuck McCann. I would learn about old movies and show business by watching *Memory Lane* with Joe Franklin. And Dad would let me stay up to watch Jack Paar, especially when crazy Jonathan Winters was on. And I would take my chair and put it next to the old black and white TV set, and I would look like I was Jack Paar's next guest. You might say, What's a young kid doing watching these sophisticated shows? It was Dad's taste. He pointed us in the right direction, and we loved it.

CHAPTER 7

Around this time Uncle Berns really entered our lives, and he would forever change them. A wild man, a Zero Mostel kind of personality, Berns was a mystical man with shoulder-length white hair, and a long white beard, a Santa Claus on acid. He could do magic tricks, and mime. He loved to be silly and make people laugh. Everyone was pulled to him, as if he were a magnet. He is an artist, and an art dealer, who actually represented Zero, who was a talented painter. Berns taught us about color and expression. He equated comedy and art. "Who's funnier than Picasso? Everyone has three eyes and six tits!"

He had his own art gallery in Manhattan, so on an occasional Sunday, we'd go visit him in the gallery, and sit with some of his painters, and listen to their stories. Berns would take us to museums, and point out the "moments" in a painting, almost as if they were movements of a symphony. It was never boring, because he was such a great teacher. Berns touched all of us in different ways. It was like we were all the best parts of him. Joel could always draw and paint, so Berns and he would sketch together. Rip could sing beautifully and Berns had a big baritone voice, so they would sing spirituals together. And Berns and I? We were just funny together. He loved to perform for anybody, never self-conscious, always totally free, a silly kind of genius, and he gave us the courage to get up and perform in almost any situation. As I think back, Dad was never threatened by our relationship with his brother. He loved seeing us play with this St. Bernard of an uncle. In a way, Berns was one of the best gifts he ever gave us.

Then one day, Dad brought home this record from the Commodore Music Shop. It was a Spike Jones record. These were novelty records. Spike would have all different kinds of sound effects, gunshots, whistles, dog barks, all perfectly integrated into his arrangements. I never heard such crazy stuff in my life. Uncle Berns said, "Lip-sync it and do it for the family." I memorized every moment of "You Always Hurt the One You Love," got it down perfectly, every whistle, gunshot and scream. They all loved it. The living room was my room now.

The three of us were always performing for the family. Rip would sing, Joel and I would do something together, and then I would close the show. It's still the best room I have ever worked. Every family event was an opening night to us. Mom would even pack our props in a small suitcase if we were going "on the road" to Grandma's house, or an uncle's home. It was expected of us.

There would be a great meal, and after the cake and cigars would be the show. We would get paid with change. My cousin Edith would give me dimes, and I would stick them on my perspiring forehead. When my forehead was full, the show was over. Mom and Dad were always the best audience.

That's how you really start. You want to make your folks laugh. Dad saw something else in us . . . we weren't just his kids, we were good. Oftentimes he would improvise with us on the tape recorder. It was so great to spend this kind of time with him. There are other ways of "having a catch." One day he came home with the record that Ernie Kovacs used for his hilarious "Nairobi Trio" routine, and three gorilla masks. The Trio were three derby-wearing apes, a piano player (me), one with two large mallets (Rip), and the leader, who had a small baton and kept time (Joel). As the piece progressed, the mallet man would turn as if he was in a music box, and slam the leader on the head with the mallets. The leader never seemed to be looking as he got hit, and couldn't understand who hit him. It was hilarious, and we did it perfectly. It was such a great feeling to do this with my big brothers. I'll never forget how excited we would be, getting into our costumes, as you could hear the relatives saying to each other, "Sit down already, the show is going to start."

Around this time, Joel developed a bad case of mono. He would actually miss two years of high school because of it, running a high fever all the time, which they couldn't get under control. He was in a tough place, sixteen years old, and homebound for so long. He took all his classes at home from tutors. Not many friends would come to visit him. He was very down, because this illness had robbed him of his high school years. So after school I would come home and we'd spend hours improvising on the tape recorder. Being funny together, watching funny people on television, and listening to comedy albums was a great medicine, maybe the only one that was working for him.

This was a particularly wonderful time for comedy records. *My Son the Folk Singer*, Jonathan Winters did a few great albums, *The First Family*, *Nichols and May Live on Broadway*, *The Button-Down Mind of Bob Newhart*, Stan Freberg's *America*, which was an original musical about American history, and the daddy of them all, *The 2,000 Year Old Man*. Mel Brooks and Carl Reiner.

This is all we did now. It was either watch a ballgame, play baseball, improvise on the tape recorder, listen to jazz, or a great "live" comedy album. They always printed that on the album jacket—"Recorded Live at the Bitter End," "Recorded Live at Carnegie Hall." Of course it was "live." Who's gonna buy "Recorded Dead at the Troubadour"? I devoured those records. I could feel the magic of being in front of an audience, just by listening to these masters. I learned about timing by listening to the way the comic would wait for the laugh to die down, and then hit the crowd with the topper. It was like surfing, riding the wave and taking it wherever it was going. Sitting on the top of it, with all of that power, gliding you almost gently to the shore only to start all over again. Not only could I hear it, I could see it, I could feel it. It really was my rock and roll.

This was an important time to be laughing. We needed laughter, because we were in the middle of the Cold War. We had a president who was an aging war hero, and a first lady too old to wear bangs. We were terrified of the Russians. It all started in 1957 with Walter Cronkite telling us, "This is the sound from Outer Space." We heard a few electronic beeps, it was Sputnik, the first satellite to orbit the earth. What the hell is this thing? Eighteen inches around with a bunch of small knitting-needle-type prongs protruding from it. We're doomed, we all thought. It's a death ray!

Nikita Khrushchev came into our lives then. A squat, scary little bald man, and his equally scary wife, and the fact that Khrushchev didn't speak English made him even scarier, so I became even more frightened of his interpreter. How did we know this interpreter was getting it right? Khrushchev came to the U.N. He took off his shoe and banged it on the table and screamed at us, "WE WILL BURY YOU!" At least, that's what they told us he said, what he really said, was, "THESE ARE NOT MY SHOES! WHO STOLE MY SHOES?"

"The Bomb" was on our minds all the time. We watched films in elementary school, showing us what nuclear explosions looked like, what they could do to a city. Horrifying. People were building fallout shelters all across the country. It wasn't a matter of *if* the Russians would bomb us, it seemed like *when*. We were practicing duck-and-cover drills in school, in case of an enemy attack. They would hurry us into the hallway, we'd sit on the floor with our arms folded, our heads down, our legs crossed. This position was surely going to save me when the Russians dropped the big one on us.

At the end of Long Beach, in a place called Lido Beach, about two miles or so from my house, was a Nike missile base. Every day at noon the air raid alarms would go off and the Nike missiles would rise up and point to the sky. You could see them from the street. I would be playing ball on the mall in front of our house, and flatbed trucks with new missiles on them would pass us. Sometimes they would stop at the light, and I would just stare at these weapons of mass destruction, and the military men guarding them, just feet from me. Terrifying.

It's also terrifying to think that we

accepted it as just the way things were. The early sixties was a stunning time. Kennedy was elected. I was thirteen, and he got me interested in politics. I thought he was amazing, a president you could relate to, and the wife was pretty cute too. Then came 1961, the summer of Maris and Mantle, Yuri Gagarin orbited the earth, the first man in space. While the Yankees were winning the pennant race, we were losing the space race. The Mercury Seven astronauts, Alan Shepard, John Glenn, were now huge stars. "We're going to go to the moon first," JFK promised. The Bay of Pigs came, the Cuban blockade, Kennedy vs. Khrushchev. The aerial photographs of the Russian missiles just ninety miles from Florida. The Russian ships bearing down on our destroyers. They will bury us! Duck and cover, duck and cover . . . At the last moment, the Russians turned back.

Terrifying. We thought the Russians were the enemy. They thought we were the enemy. And we were both wrong. It's the French.

And then Dad brought home an album called *Bill Cosby Is a Very Funny Fellow, Right!* I loved Bill Cosby. I thought Bill was the greatest comedian of that time, and the most important one to me. I could relate to Cosby. He had brothers. I had brothers. He played ball at Temple. I belonged to a temple. So there was a bond.

On that album—I think it's the finest piece of recorded comedy ever—is a routine called "Noah," and it's about the building of the Ark. It was an amazing piece. So I took that recording, and I memorized it, and I did it in the school show called "The Swing Show" at Long Beach High School. It was a variety show . . . a big band, singers, and I was the comic. And it was the only time that my dad ever got to see me perform in a sport jacket, "live," in front of an audience that wasn't relatives.

I was a smash. Well, I was doing Cosby's stuff, but I didn't think that I was stealing. I was fourteen years old. I just did it word for word in front of an audience. Is that stealing? In Hollywood, they call that an homage. And then years later, friends were now listening to Cosby and they'd say to me, "Billy, there's this guy, Cosby. He's doing your stuff!"

I loved being in front of audiences. It always felt like one of the safest places for me to be. Fielding ground balls, and being on a stage, that's where I really felt most at home. My friends would come over and listen to these records. One of them, Joel Robins, would become my comedy partner. He was hilarious. A moon face, with great

145

timing. We started doing things together. We would imitate Laurel and
Hardy, derby hats and all the trimmings,
and do their routines and others we
would come up with. We lip-synced the
entire Stan Freberg *America* album,
over an hour long, playing all the characters, perfectly lip-syncing all of the
songs. He and I performed together at
sweet sixteens, "The Swing Show," in
the hallway, and basically at the drop of
a laugh. Comedy was becoming more
and more important to me. If I couldn't
be the Yankees' shortstop, I was going
to be a comedian. Or better yet, the
funniest shortstop the Yankees ever
had.

Uncle Milt was always my mentor.
He always had great advice and stories
of the giants that he was working with
at Decca Records. Uncle Milt always
made sure to take the time to tell me
something that would inspire me. He

never discouraged me. Never said, "It's a tough business. Have something to fall back on." He always made me feel that I could be funny anyplace, not just the living room. He'd say, "Listen, Billy. I'm producing a guy now. I think he's a genius. You must watch him. His name is Sammy Davis, Jr. He can do everything. He sings great, he dances better than anybody, and he does great impressions. If you want to be a performer, great, but try to do a lot of things. Not just one thing. Watch Sammy Davis, Jr."

Ironically, Sammy was the star of the first Broadway show that I ever saw, *Mr. Wonderful*, which also starred Jack Carter. Dad got tickets from his friend, *The Daily News* critic Douglas Watt, and we sat in the front row. I remember the house lights coming down, the orchestra playing the overture, and then Sammy walking out to a great ovation, and I also remember feeling I wanted it to be me.

I watched Sammy every chance I got, never once thinking that someday I not only would become his opening act, but that I would also become Sammy Davis, Jr. Opening for Sammy was the greatest thrill, we became good friends, and I would watch his show every night. We did three weeks together at Harrah's hotel, in Lake Tahoe. I went on at 8:00 P.M., and I would get to the dressing room, around 7:00 or so. Sammy had been there since 6:00. I would always go in to say hello, and we'd play backgammon and talk. The stories he would tell were priceless. He was mesmerizing. Listening to his history and firsthand accounts of the biggest stars in the business was simply sensational . . . that's how I developed my impression of him. I couldn't help but absorb him, and many a night I would leave his dressing room with his sound, his inflections, his "thing," man, ringing in my head. And Sammy could do something I never could do. He could tap-dance with both legs.

But then I discovered something that made me forget Sammy, made me forget Cosby, made me forget *The 2,000 Year Old Man*, made me forget the Yankees, made me forget everything that I cared about because I discovered my penis. This was the greatest discovery of all. I discovered mine six, seven, eight, ten times a day. I wonder what the record is. The penis is not a good thing to get addicted to. Let's face it. It's a weapon of self-destruction and you don't need U.N. inspectors to find it. You know right where it is every second.

This little guy has caused problems for men throughout history. The great Thomas Jefferson had affairs. His boyhood friend Strom Thurmond—same thing. Kennedy, Eisenhower, Clinton . . . all men of power, and the power went right to their pants. Even FDR fooled around. This I don't understand. Because if you have a chance to screw Eleanor Roosevelt every night of the week, where you going? A great woman, without a doubt, but not really a "hottie." He actually faked being paralyzed so he wouldn't have to have sex with her. He wasn't only frightened of fear itself, he was frightened of that overbite. Now I had the same problem, right in the palm of my hand.

I was so horny. I was always ready. My glands were relentless. They were screaming at me.

NOW, NOW, NOW!

And I was ready for anything that looked hump-able. A bagel.

NOW!

It was poppy-seeded, I almost shredded myself to death.

A 45 RPM record.

NOW!

To this day I can't look Lesley Gore in the eye.

NOW, NOW, NOW!

And then I saw The Girl.

NOW!

This wasn't lust.

BULLSHIT!

No, it wasn't. This was something different. This was love.

COME ON, YOU'RE TALKING TO ME NOW!

I fell in love with this adorable blond girl. First love. The kind of love that actually hurts. She was the cutest thing I'd ever seen. I knew what head-over-heels meant because I kept tripping and falling when I would follow her home from school.

THIS IS SO FUCKING BORING!

Finally, I got up enough nerve to ask her out and she said yes.

LET'S GET READY TO RUMBLE!

My first date. Panic. I walked to her house. (Driving was still years away.) She lived in Lido Beach, not far from the Nike missile beach. A perfect image for my condition. I was so nervous I couldn't remember where she lived.

MAKE A LEFT!

It was the first global positioning system.

YOU HAVE ARRIVED AT YOUR DESTINATION!

Leave me alone!

NEVER! I OWN YOU!

I got to the door, I started to knock and I heard something that scared the hell out of me.

LET ME RING THE BELL!

I didn't know what to do, I just stood there frozen.

FORGET IT. I'LL KNOCK!

And if they hadn't cut off the top six to eight inches, I would have leveled the place . . .

So now we start going out, and it was the first time I made out with somebody in a movie theater, in the balcony of the Laurel Theatre in Long Beach.

NOW!

Then in the back seat of a friend's car . . .

NOW!

Oh, she was Miss Right . . .

NOW!

And I got up enough nerve and I said, "You know what? I love you, I really do . . . Let's go steady."

"Oh, no, Billy I can't do that. As a matter of fact, I don't want to go out with you anymore. I really just like you as a friend."

OH NO!

153

"Really?"

"I mean, I like you, but not in that way . . ."

"Uh-huh . . ." I understand. (But my glands don't.)

WHAT ABOUT ME?

Dad's other secret life

CHAPTER 8

The rejection was too much to take. The first time out, and you open yourself up to someone. You tell somebody that you care about them, you tell somebody how you feel about them, and they say, "I just don't like you." That hurts. I was mad. I was embarrassed. I felt like a fool. I was fifteen, and I was ready to settle down, and have a family. It felt so right, how could I have been so wrong? Why didn't she like me? I couldn't see straight for days. I didn't eat, I didn't sleep. I didn't think about anything else but The Girl. It was a Tuesday night . . .

October 15, 1963. I was sitting at the kitchen table studying for a chemistry test in the morning, and I didn't give a shit. I had just lost The Girl. Who cared about chemistry? Was chemistry ever going to be important in my life? No. Was I ever going to need chemistry? No. I knew what I was going to be. I didn't need chemistry. Was anyone ever going to say to me, "Billy, what's lead?" And I wouldn't hesitate and look him right in the eye and proudly say, "Pb."

"Yes, it is, Bill. Yes, it is. Here's a million dollars."

That was never going to happen. And every time I'd turn the page of the chemistry book, I'd see The Girl's face.

My parents came into the kitchen to say goodbye. They were on their way out to their Tuesday night bowling league at Long Beach Bowl. They loved bowling with their friends. They had so much fun doing it. And frankly, this was pretty much the only fun that they were having now because times had changed for us, and not for the better.

The Commodore Music Shop had closed a few years earlier. It couldn't keep up with the discount record places that were springing up around Manhattan. That big Sam Goody's by the Chrysler Building opened, and our little store was right across the street, and Goody's just swallowed us up like a whale and a minnow. All those decades of great music and musicians and laughs and legends were gone, in the name of progress. *The New York Times* did a front-page story on the closing with a picture of Dad and Uncle Milt, Henry "Red" Allen, and Eddie Condon, playing one last riff in the now empty store. "Man, this is the end of an era," they wrote.

And the bands that I loved, the music of Coleman Hawkins, Lester Young, Sidney Bechet, Ben Webster, Roy Eldridge, Conrad Janis and the Tailgaters, and all the others, were replaced now by the Duprees, the Earls, the Shirelles and the Beach Boys. These original American jazz giants, the men, and women, who gave birth to all the rest of our music, were now reduced to playing outside ballparks with garters on their sleeves, wearing straw hats.

My dad now was fifty-four years old, and he was scared. With Joel and Rip away at college, he was out of a job. Oh, he did the sessions on Friday and Saturday nights, but he gave most of that money to the musicians to keep them going. Dad was also closing down the Commodore label, working out of the pressing plant in Yonkers. It was so sad to see him struggle this way. Nobody wanted to hear this music anymore.

160

Sundays weren't fun that summer. Joel, Rip and I would go to the plant to help him box up the very last Commodore album, a Lester Young re-issue. The newly pressed records came down a conveyer belt, we put them in their jackets, then sealed them in plastic, put them in cartons, then into the trunk of the Belvedere, and delivered them ourselves to record stores. It was tough.

Dad was exhausted, and sad. Jazz was his best friend, and it was dying, and he knew he couldn't save it. One day, a man came to the house, and Pop sold him his personal complete set of Commodore originals. I think he got $500 for them. And as the man took them away . . . It was the only time I ever saw my father cry.

That August, Dad was suffering from double vision in one of his eyes. They decided to put him in the hospital to run some tests. I don't remember him even having a cold, so this felt very threatening. We stood in the driveway as Mom and Dad walked to the Belvedere, which was parked on the street, his small suitcase in one hand, his other arm around her. He wore a patch over the bad eye, and when they got to the car, Dad stopped and handed Mom the keys, sheepishly opened the passenger door and got in. He let her drive. I knew something bad was going to happen.

When he walked into the kitchen that October night, he looked worried. He looked upset. And when he saw me pining away for The Girl, he looked mad. We had just finished a month of Sundays together. With my brothers away at college, I didn't have to share him. It was just the two of us for the first time . . .

There was one Sunday I remember in particular. It was October 6 of 1963. On that black and white TV set, we watched Sandy Koufax and the Los Angeles Dodgers sweep the Yankees in the 1963 World Series. I was so depressed. I couldn't believe it, sitting there and watching Koufax and Drysdale and Maury Wills celebrate their four-game "dis-Mantling" of the Yankees. "Dad, I can't believe this. How could the Yankees lose four straight?"

And he said, "Don't worry about it. It will never happen again."

But that night in the kitchen, as I blankly stared at my chemistry book, he started yelling at me.

"Billy, look at you. Look at you. You're going to have to get your grades up. You'd better study because I can't afford to send you to school. That's how it's going to work, kid. You understand? You get your grades up, maybe get some sort of scholarship or something, and you're going to go. Don't you understand what's happening here? I don't know how I'm going to be able to send

Joel and Rip anymore. You're going to have to get some sort of scholarship or something." He continued, the intensity in his voice growing.

"Look at you moping around. This is all because of that goddamn girl, isn't it?"

I snapped, "What the hell do you know?"

It flew out of my mouth. I never spoke to him like that. Ever. He looked at me, rage in his eyes. I was scared, didn't know what to do. I froze. He was quiet now, the words measured . . .

"Don't talk to me like that, please."
And they left.

I felt awful. Oh, why did I say that? I ran after him to apologize, but they were in the car and gone before I could get there. I came back to the kitchen thinking, okay, calm down, they'll be home around 11:30, quarter to twelve. I'll apologize then, and maybe he'd help me study for this test. This whole thing was because of The Girl. I studied for another thirty minutes or so staring at the chemistry book. "That's it. That's all," I said to myself as I shut the book, knowing I was going to take it on the chin. I went to my room in the back. And before I got into bed, I closed the door, but not all the way. I don't like the dark. I left a little bit of light from the hallway coming through, and I fell asleep.

I was startled by the sound of the front door opening, and I looked at the clock, and it was 11:30, just like always, and I could hear Mom coming down the hallway toward the back of the house, where the bedrooms were, and just like always, she was hysterical laughing . . . or so I thought. I was still waking up, when I realized she wasn't laughing at all. She was crying . . . and it got louder and louder and *louder* and LOUDER and *LOUDER* and *LOUDER*.

The door flew open. The light blinded me, further confusing me, and she was on me in a second.

"Billy, Billy, Daddy's gone. Daddy's gone. Daddy's gone."

Uncle Danny was with her. They spoke at the same time, but I only heard one thing.

"Dad's gone, kid. He didn't have a chance."

"Daddy's gone."

"Dad is dead."

"Daddy's dead."

"Dad is dead."

I didn't know what they were talking about. I was so confused. I thought they were talking about their father. I said, "Grandpa died?"

Mom held my face tenderly and she said, "Billy, no. Listen to me. Listen to me.

Darling. Dad had a heart attack at the bowling alley and he didn't make it. They tried to save him, and they couldn't. He's gone. He died there, Billy. He didn't come home with me. He's gone. Daddy's gone."

She sat down on the bed next to me, and I put my arm around her. And the first thing I said to her was, "Mom, I will always take care of you, always."

Then she looked at me, her red eyes glistening and said, simply, "Oh, Billy . . ." And she laid her head on my shoulder.

"I've got to call Joel. I've got to call Rip and tell them. Billy, how am I going to tell them that Dad's gone? How am I going to tell them? Help me find the words. Get dressed. Your uncles are coming over. It's going to be a long night. We've got a lot of planning to do. I'm sorry this happened, darling. I'm just so sorry."

She kissed my cheek and she held me for a few seconds. I could feel her warm tears on my cheek, some of them cascading down my face and falling on my thigh. She and Danny left, leaving me alone in the room. I looked in the mirror, and I didn't see a kid anymore. It was as if someone had handed me a boulder, a huge boulder that I would have to carry around for the rest of my life.

I went to the dining room. Her brothers, my uncles, were there, Milt, Danny, Barney. We all held hands with Mom trying to make sense out of what had just happened to us, just an hour before.

And the confusion was heightened by the red lobster scope spinning on the roof of the police car, which had pulled up in front of the house. The red light was flying around the living room, bouncing off the large mirror that was over the couch, and before I knew it, there was a police officer in the house. We never had a cop in the house before. It's scary. Big guy in a blue uniform with a big gun. The sound of his leather boots on the living room floor.

He took off his hat, and I remember feeling surprised that he was bald. He kept apologizing for the timing of all of this. As he walked over to us, he got bigger and bigger. He stood right above me, the red light dancing behind him, and he handed me a manila envelope.

"What's this?"

"That's your dad's belongings, son. I'm sorry."

I opened it up, and it was simply his baseball hat, his wedding ring, his watch and his wallet. A man's whole life in a manila envelope?

I had never held his wallet before, never. When you're a kid, you never get money from your dad. You always get

169

money from your mom. "Mom, I need money."

"My purse is there, dear. Take what you want."

A father never said, "Here's my wallet. Take what you want."

And I opened it for the very first time. It was simply his driver's license and pictures of us. His wallet, dark brown leather, worn on the edges, was like some sort of holy book. I had never seen these photos of us before. Joel, Rip and I, from different times in our lives, carefully assembled. The last one was a simple photo of Mom, around the time they met—young, beautiful, timeless. I closed it, and never opened it again.

Ceil Weinstein lived next door. There was a hedge between the two homes about six feet high and four feet wide, so you very rarely saw Ceil, but you always heard her. She was a big woman with a very shrill voice and a laugh like an electrical storm, except now she was frightened.

"Helen, what is a police car doing out there? Is everything okay? Why are the police there?"

"Ceil, it's the worst news. Jack died tonight. He had a heart attack at the bowling alley and they couldn't save him. He's gone. He's gone. Jack is gone."

Her anguished voice stabbed through the fall night.

"No, Helen. No, no. Who's going to take Billy to the ballgames?"

Uncle Milt stayed in my room with me that night. He slept in Rip's bed. Rip and I always shared that back room. I never had my own room, until I started going out on the road after I got married . . . Uncle Milt was great that night. He took charge, taking care of his sister, helping her make all the funeral arrangements. I remember feeling a little awkward as he undressed. I mean, on the night you're told your father is gone, the last thing you want to see is your chubby uncle in his boxer shorts. We talked all night, the moonlight trickling through the window, giving Milt a blue tint as he reassured me he would always be there for me.

When Jack met Helen...1937

CHAPTER 9

The next day the strangest thing happened. The car wouldn't start. The gray-on-gray Plymouth Belvedere refused to go. He had driven this car a hundred miles a day every day for all the years that he had it. He took perfect care of it. It never failed him until this day. It knew that he was gone, and it refused to go without him—it just stood in the driveway with the hood up.

And Stan, the service man from the local gas station, was trying to start it. He and Dad had worked on the car for years together (and "Nellie" before that), and they'd kept it running perfectly. He was a stocky guy with blond hair, blue eyes, a jumpsuit, his name written over his heart. He always had a smile, and a big hearty laugh. But now Stan had tears in his eyes as he tried to jump the battery and the battery wouldn't take the jump. He kept trying, over and over again.

I stood on the grass, watching. I couldn't believe what I was seeing. I started having flashes of what I imagined happened to my dad, the night before, in the bowling alley as the medical people worked on him, trying to get him started too. The images swirling together through my mind, paralyzing me with their vivid intensity . . .

EVERYBODY GET BACK!

CLEAR!

And I'd see Dad not breathing . . . the car not starting.

CLEAR!

The battery not taking the charge, Stan crying: "Try it again!"

Someone pounding on Dad's chest . . .

CLEAR!

People holding Mom back as she screams, "No! No! No!"

CLEAR!

And as Stan towed the Belvedere away, the grille of the car looked sad.

Joel came home. Rip came home. It was just the four of us now. There would be no more Sundays. And they told us that night we were going to view the body. Because the Jews bury very quickly. Very quickly. I had an uncle who was a narcoleptic, and he'd nod off and you'd hear digging. One summer they buried him five times.

I wish there was some way that you could edit people out of your life. Like it was a movie. People who come into moments both happy and sad, and you don't want them there, and they're stuck in your memory forever. But if it was a movie, you could cut them out. Cut him out. He doesn't belong in the scene. Cut her. She doesn't belong in this moment.

The person that I wanted to cut out was the funeral director at the funeral home, which ironically was in the shadows of Yankee Stadium in the Bronx. My life had just fallen apart. Why did I have to talk to this guy? He was an odd-looking chubby man, with a terrible speech impediment that made him sound like Sylvester the Cat. He pinned a black mourning ribbon on us all. They cut it, and then he chanted the Jewish prayer for the dead, which for this guy was a total disaster. He was spitting all over us. The more serious he got, the funnier it became to me. Lines, jokes were flying into my brain. I looked at my brother Joel. He knew what I was thinking, and he mouthed silently . . .

"Don't."

There must have been hundreds of great musicians there, all there to say goodbye to their great friend. The four of us just walked through them. They didn't say a word. They just bowed their heads out of respect. And then the four of us now were led into the private viewing room and there was Dad. What a cruel fate, that the first dead person I saw in my life was my father. And it didn't look like him. He was so still. Just hours before we were arguing about The Girl. And I kept thinking: Is this my fault? Did I make this happen? Did our fight bring this on? Why didn't I get a chance to say I was sorry? Why didn't I get a chance to say goodbye?

But he was so still. I got up enough

courage to follow Mom closer, I saw that he had this terrible bruise on his forehead that they couldn't repair, and I felt awful that he had been hurt before he died.

What had happened was, Mom told me later, he had made a very difficult spare the night before. The last thing my dad did on earth was make the four, seven, ten. It's a tough spare to make, and he was so happy. "Whoa, Helen. Look at that. What a day . . ."

And he dropped dead, just like that. His head hit the scoring table, the floor . . . it didn't matter because in my denial, I was more upset that he hurt his head, totally forgetting the fact that he was gone.

Aunt Sheila was behind me.

"Billy, darling. He's just sleeping, dear. That's all. He's just sleeping. See how nice? Daddy's just sleeping."

I couldn't believe what I was hearing. I turned, furious. "Wake him up. I thought he was dead. Go ahead. Wake him up . . .

"Let's get the fuck out of here. This place gives me the creeps."

She looked at me for a long time . . . "Leonard, get the car."

The funeral was the next day, and it was jammed. It seemed like all of those great musicians who posed for that famous photo, *A Great Day in Harlem*, were there. My dad's mother, Grandma Sophie, couldn't contain herself. His sister, Marcia, was consoling her, and then Uncle Berns walked in. He had been in Mexico, and had flown all night. Berns, our giant, couldn't contain himself. Seeing him cry at the sight of his "big brother" was profound. He shuddered and moaned with sadness, holding the three of us, his brother's sons, in his massive arms. Sophie, speaking only in her native Russian, was wailing Dad's name, a mother screaming in pain for her lost child. I felt like I was in someone else's life. Nothing made sense to me. Every second was excruciating. All the relatives, that I only knew laughing, were now all crying, shock and despair on everyone's face. I never felt so alone in my life, and then I looked up, and three of my friends, Michael Stein, David Beller, and Joel Robins, walked in.

They had made their way to the Bronx to be with me. Michael had lost his mother, two years before, so he knew what I was going through. He had the same look in his eye that I had now. I couldn't believe that they came. We all hugged, and when Mom saw them, she shook her head in wonder, and said, "Friends, such good friends." I will always love them for coming.

After the service, we were driven to the cemetery, which is in New Jersey. We passed Yankee Stadium on our way. It seemed only right, I thought. Everyone gathered at the family plot, which until that day I didn't know existed. Grandpa Julius had purchased this plot for all of his family we were told. "Someday everyone will be here," Uncle Mac said. "Thanks for the good news," I thought to myself. I stood there looking at all of my older relatives, thinking to myself, "Why Dad?" The service at the grave was the hardest part. Seeing the freshly dug grave, roots protruding from its walls, the coffin in place, following Mom, we tossed flowers, and then shovels of dirt on the casket, the sound of it hitting, slicing like a razor blade into my soul. What had felt so unreal before was now brutally true.

I looked at everyone as they mourned, their sobs and sniffles mixing with the birds singing in the trees. Willie "The Lion" Smith caught my eye, and he nodded, and continued praying in Hebrew. Just past the crowd, I saw

183

three gravediggers, in workclothes, lean-
ing on their shovels. One of them was
looking at his watch.

After the funeral, everyone came
back to the house. There must have
been hundreds of family members,
neighbors, friends, and a lot of food and
conversation to keep your mind off it
during the mourning period. It's called
a Shiva. But to me, the right word is
"shiver" because the feeling of Pop's
death just made me tremble all the
time. They make the mourners sit on
these hard little wooden stools. Who
the hell came up with this one? Isn't it
bad enough what has happened to us?
Why do we have to suffer more? Aunt
Sheila was upset that we covered the
mirrors, a Jewish tradition, while I was
upset that we didn't cover Sheila. People kept saying the same thing to me,
"It'll take time, you'll see, it'll take time."
Grandpa couldn't take it anymore. After

hearing this for the umpteenth time, he turned to me and said, "Time is a bastard: When you're sad there's too much of it, and when you're happy there's never enough."

And the whole feeling in the house, this house that was always filled with laughter and jazz, was now just so sad and dark. I stayed in my room. I didn't come out. I didn't want to see anybody. Friends would come over to try to talk to me, try to make me feel better, you know, but . . . I was one of the first of my friends to lose a parent. Nobody really knows what to say to you. Hell, we were fifteen. We didn't know what to say about a lot of stuff. I didn't come out. A living room filled with people, and I didn't care. I stayed in my room, and I realized I still hadn't cried.

And then one day, I heard laughter. Big laughs. Everybody having a great time. I had to come out to see who was

185

working my room. And it was my crazy Uncle Berns. Performing for the family. He was making everybody laugh, even my mother was smiling. He was carrying on, making everybody else feel a little bit better, and taking some of the pain out of his heart as well. Berns was making people forget just for a few moments why they were there, and it was okay. He had just lost his brother, the person he was closest to in the world. And the message to me was profound because it meant that even in your worst pain it's still okay to laugh.

And then one day, Wild Bill Davidson came over. And he sat down, and he took out his trumpet and played the blues. Then Edmond Hall came over and took out his clarinet, and he played the most beautiful version of "My Buddy." And Arvel Shaw came over and Eddie Condon, Tyree Glenn, Willie "The Lion" Smith, Zutty Singleton, and there was a jam session in a Shiva house that people will never, ever forget. Even my mom was tapping her foot. Because once you hear the music, you can't stand still.

Then it comes time for everybody to go back to their lives, including an old friend . . . The gravelly voice, the moist eyes, the scent of bourbon . . .

"Hey, Face. It's going to be all right, Face. It's going to be all right . . . How do you know you never going to see him again, Face? We don't know what this is."

I wasn't sure what he meant.

"Face, consider the rose. The rose is the sweetest-smelling flower of all, and it's the most beautiful because it's the most simple, right . . . ? But sometimes, Face, you got to clip the rose. You got to cut the rose back, so something sweeter-smelling and stronger and even more beautiful will grow in its place. You see?

"Now you may not understand that now, Face, but someday you will. I guarantee it. Someday, Face, you're going to consider the rose. Can you dig that . . . ? I knew that you could."

Someone handed me a boulder

CHAPTER 10

*J*oel left first. He had to go back to college, the University of Miami. Rip went back to the University of Bridgeport. Hard goodbyes. It was just me and Mom now.

Uncle Mac took me aside. "Billy, don't take this personal, but your brothers are gone now, you got to be the man of the house. That's your job."

Aunt Sheila, pinching my cheek . . . "Billy, darling, we're so proud of you. Be strong for Mommy, okay? You're the man of the house. That's your job."

191

I didn't want the job.

Then after everybody's gone, you're left with it. You're left with the shit of it, the size of it, this opponent in your life, this hole in your heart that you can't possibly repair fast enough. And the first thing that happens to you is you get angry. You get so mad that this has happened to you at this point in your life, you want answers. I was so furious I could storm right into God's office.

"Excuse me. I would like to see him . . . No, I don't have an appointment, but . . . What is your name . . . ? Peter what . . . ? Leviiine?"

I feel his presence. "There you are! How could you do this? How could you do this to her? Why would you do this to us . . . ?

"You move in mysterious ways? I can't believe you actually said that! You call yourself a fair God? Really? If you're fair, then why would you take him, but you leave Mengele out there? How is that fair? Why would you do this to me? WHY?

"It's the hand I'm dealt? The cards I get to play? Oh, that's just great. Are you God or some blackjack dealer? I mean, Jesus Christ! How could you say . . . Oh, hi. I didn't see you there. You look great. No. I didn't recognize you with your arms down. You look great. Went into business with the old man, huh . . . ? Well, maybe I wanted to do that too.

"You know what? I will never believe in you. How can I? Look what you've done to me. I will have other gods before you. There should be an Eleventh Commandment. Thou shalt not be a schmucky god . . . I'm sorry. I'm sorry." I turn to leave, but I can't . . . "Would you do me one favor, please? When you see him, would you tell him that I passed the chemistry test?"

*   *   *

Getting back to school was so hard because I had this boulder to take with me everyplace. But then I developed something else. The best way I can describe it is by what I called it. I called it the "otherness" because that's how I felt. I wasn't here. I wasn't there. I was in an other place. A place where you look, but you don't really see, a place where you hear but you don't really listen. It was "the otherness" of it all.

I pushed the boulder up the hallway in school. Friends flying by me having a great old time. Some of them staring at that stupid black mourning ribbon I was wearing. I looked like I had won a contest for making the very worst pie. People either avoided me, or they looked at me in a strange way.

I thought I knew what they were thinking: "There's the kid whose father died in a FUCKING BOWLING ALLEY!" I would feel angry at Dad, embarrassed, because he died there. This isn't how it should be. You should die in bed with all your family around you, smiling at each of your loved ones, telling them you love them, and that it's okay. You're ready, and not afraid, and don't be sad, didn't we have a great life? And with them almost rooting you on to the next place, you leave this earth—that's how it should be, not dying on the floor of a bowling alley surrounded by people wearing rented, multicolored shoes. I was seething . . . at my life, and that I felt that way.

And then I'd see The Girl with The New Boyfriend. Blond-haired, blue-eyed football player, Impala-driving, Nazi bastard. And I'd get confused. I'd get so confused sometimes. I didn't know what I felt worse about, the fact that my father was gone or that I didn't get The Girl. I'd feel so guilty. I'd feel so torn apart. I mean, who was I grieving for? Was I grieving for him, or was I grieving for me?

Basketball tryouts. The sign was posted in the hallway. I wanted to be on the varsity basketball team. That was the glamour team. The whole town would come out for the Friday night games. I played three years of varsity baseball in high school and the only people who came to the games were the players. I had made *junior* varsity basketball the year before, but I had to make the varsity team because my brother Rip had been on the varsity, and I wanted to do whatever he did because I thought he was the coolest (except for the kicking leg). I also had to do something just to get out of the house.

It was probably too soon for me because the first day of tryouts, somebody threw me the ball, and it bounced right

196

past me. I just couldn't see it. I would dribble the ball off my foot because I was in some other place. The otherness was blinding me. The ball kept going places I didn't want it to go. I couldn't guard anybody. I couldn't keep up because I had this boulder to take with me everyplace I went. Three days of trying out for the team, total disaster, total. Embarrassing play.

After the third day of this, the coach, Gene Farry, called me into his office after practice, I thought to cut me. Instead, he asked me something that nobody had asked me since October 15.

"Bill, are you okay? How's everything at home?"

I stared at him, unable to speak. Suddenly, tears welled up in my eyes. I just exploded . . . the words, making their way out of my heart . . .

"I'm sorry. I'm sorry, Coach. I'm sorry.

197

"There's nobody home.

"I am so lonely.

"I don't know what I'm doing from one second to the next.

"I'm failing every subject.

"I just don't know anymore.

"There's nobody home. You know what I do after school every day, Coach? I run home and I cook. I make dinner for my mother because she's out looking for work. She's out trying to get a job, and I want to have food on the table when she comes home, so she won't have to do it herself.

"And she looks so sad and so tired. And I try to make her laugh, but that's not working either.

"And I'm trying to keep up. I'm really trying to keep up with my studies but I can't. I go into my room in the back, and every time I open a book, I can hear her in the next room.

"I can hear her moaning and sobbing

198

herself to sleep every night because the walls are too fucking thin."

The tears ran down my face like they were escaping from prison, the wetness of them oddly reassuring. I wasn't embarrassed. Coach Farry, only twenty-four at the time, smiled at me, and said, "Take all the time you need, I'll be out here."

He put me on the team. That's the nicest thing anyone has ever done for me.

We have our first game. It's an away game at a school on the Island called East Rockaway High School, and I'm sitting in the bleachers watching the JV game, which preceded the varsity game. I'm sitting there all alone, except for my boulder, looking but not seeing, hearing but not listening. Two friends are behind me, Harvey and Joe.

Now our fans are arriving at the away game. And as they drift into the gymnasium to watch the game, Harvey innocently says to Joe, "Hey, your father's here."

And I stood up and said, "Where?" I thought they were talking to me.

I couldn't believe it happened, but it did. I didn't know what to do. It was just . . . out there. What could I do? I mean, I couldn't turn around. What was I going to say? "Sorry guys, I thought my dead father just walked into the gym to watch me play"? So I just sat down as if nothing had happened, just staring straight ahead but not seeing, listening but not hearing. I couldn't imagine what was going on behind me . . .

I didn't talk to Harvey again for the rest of high school. If I saw him coming down the hallway, I went the other way.

The next week was November 22, 1963. Another Jack died.

Now the whole country had the

otherness, except I had a double dip. And this misery continued for all of us for years and years, with a president from Texas who we really didn't like and a war that we really couldn't win . . .

And then one Sunday night in February of 1964, Mom and I were watching the Ed Sullivan show. Because that's how I spent every Sunday night now, just she and I watching Ed Sullivan. And something great happened for the country, something that made everybody forget what a hellhole the world was becoming. The Beatles were on Ed Sullivan. And for the first time in months, I smiled. And for the first time in my life, I liked another kind of music. And all through this magical broadcast, I heard this ticking noise. No. It wasn't *60 Minutes*. It was Mom, making that disapproving sound. I was seeing the Beatles. She was seeing the death of jazz.

Oh, I wanted to be like one of the

Beatles. If I could be like one of the Beatles, maybe I could get The Girl.

Once a month I got my hair cut from this wonderful barber in Long Beach. Remember barbers? His name was Cosmo. He cut everybody's hair. There was always a wait for Cosmo. I would sit in the chair. He'd put the smock around me. And I'd say to him, "Cosmo, leave it long in the back, okay? Long in the back."

"Sure, Bill. Like one of the Be-ah tuls, huh? Everybody wants to look like one of the Be-ah tuls. You will look like a Be-ah tul too."

He then started to clip my hair off . . .

"What are you doing!"

"Your mother called."

At the end of my junior year, something good finally happened for us. Joel graduated college and got a job teaching art in the very, very same junior high school that we all had gone to in Long Beach (he had become a really wonderful artist). He decided to live at home and give Mom most of his salary. So a little bit of the pressure was off Mom now. Until the draft board made Joel 1a, ready for induction. The buildup was starting in Viet Nam, and the army wanted him. Mom wouldn't let them take him. She made an impassioned speech in front of the military draft board pleading her case, that Joel was now the head of the household, with two younger brothers to support. She won, and Joel was spared.

Then came my senior year in high school. This time I made the basketball team the way I wanted to make it. I worked at it all summer. I was playing baseball wherever I could, but at night I worked on my shot, on my defense, my passing, and I played a lot that year. We were a very good team, the Long Beach Marines of 1965, and there's one game that they always talk about. This was the game we played against Erasmus Hall High from Brooklyn.

They were a fantastic high school basketball team. They were the number two high school team in the entire country. The number one team was from the City, a team named Power Memorial. And their center was Lew Alcindor. Eventually, he becomes Abdul-Jabbar. (In between he was Izzy Itzkowitz, for about three weeks. He said the food was too gassy, and he felt guilty, so he became a Muslim. We almost had him.)

One of our coaches had played at Erasmus, and knew their coach, and they arranged a special exhibition game, and mighty Erasmus, a predominantly black team, agrees to come out to Long Island to play us, a mostly white middle- to upper-middle-class school, in a predomi-

nantly Jewish town. This is unheard of—
a City team to play a Long Island team?
It was big news in the local papers, almost like the Knicks were coming. I
mean, Custer had better odds in Vegas
than we did.

Erasmus terrified us by the way they
arrived at our school. They show up at
our school in a Greyhound bus for the
team, and another bus for the children
of the team. We're in the locker room before the game having our legs waxed
and—well, it's a home game, you want
to look good. And Coach Farry comes in
and says, "Listen, guys. Erasmus is a great
team. But we're pretty good too, so let's
show 'em who we are. Take the court.
Come on, Marines, fight."

We run out there. It's our home
court. We're greeted by a thousand Erasmus fans, stuffed into their side of the
gym, and they're all in dashikis, African
tops. This was a terrible time for whites

205

and blacks in America. The South was literally exploding: dogs biting, people rioting, churches with children in them blown to bits, buses burning, civil rights workers murdered, "Blood on the leaves, blood at the root." Black people were starting to turn back to their African roots. The heavyweight champion had changed his name from Cassius Clay to Cassius X and then finally to Muhammad Ali. It was an edgy, scary time.

The Erasmus crowd was on their feet now, as their team warmed up. Even the cheerleaders could dunk. They're swaying back and forth, their arms waving back and forth in these choreographed African-feeling chants: "Erasmus, Erasmus. KILL THEM."

And our cheerleaders were on the other side of the court singing (to the tune of Hava Negilah), "Please don't hurt our players. They're very nice boys, and they bruise easily. OY!"

So we're down 55 points as the second quarter begins, and I'm just sitting there. My mom's in the stands. She came to every game, and every game that we fell behind, she did the same thing. Yell at the coach.

"Put Crystal in. Let's go coach. Number 11. We can't be any further behind. Let's go. Let everybody play. I pay a lot of taxes in this school system, and I—"

Oh, God. Coach Farry turned to me and said something that terrifies me to this day.

"Go in."

"Are you nuts? There's a *game* going on here."

So I check into the game. All of my friends in Long Beach stand up, and give me a standing ovation, and they wouldn't stop. My friend David Sherman had nicknamed me "The Brute" because I had won the intramural wrestling championship . . . 122

pounds of steel. In the middle of this ovation he starts chanting, "BRUTE, BRUTE, BRUTE," and everyone follows him.

I walked out onto the court, like a Christian in the Roman Colosseum. They wouldn't stop. "BRUTE, BRUTE, BRUTE!" I couldn't imagine what Erasmus was thinking: *This* is their secret weapon? So I tried to walk like I was six eight. I looked at that Erasmus team with an attitude. I tucked in my jersey with authority . . . and my number disappeared into my trunks. It's hard to be intimidating when your nipples are showing.

Play resumes, and I'm guarding a building in a pair of socks. This is the biggest man I've ever seen in my life, he has his own climate. He's running upcourt, and I'm guarding him and he's laughing at me.

"Hey, where you from, Oz?"

This guy was so big, his crucifix had a real man on it.

He'd dribble the ball up high, taunting me. "Hey, munchkin. Come on, munchkin. Take the ball from me, munchkin."

So I get pissed off. I see an opening, and I knock the ball loose. It rolls on the court. I dive on it. He dives on it. The ref goes, "Jump ball!"

We get to center court. Everyone's hysterical laughing. Both sides of the gym are united now about one thing: I look like a schmuck. He's up there. I'm down here. We look like a semicolon. He doesn't even have to jump to win the tip. I've got my head hanging down because I'm now a sight gag.

Everybody's laughing. Then I heard that voice in the stands. "Come on, Crystal! Come on, 11! Give it your best shot! Let's go!"

And she was right. What a great

credo. Give it your best shot. Simple, but powerful. Give it your best shot. So with a renewed confidence, I looked up . . . into his crotch . . . and said, "This is ridiculous."

The ref stepped in, still laughing. "Let's go guys, jump ball." *Give it your best shot. Give it your best shot. Give it your best shot*. The ref threw up the ball, and then everything was in slow motion for me. I remember the ball spinning. I could read it in the gym lights, Spaaaalllldiiiiing.

Give it your best shot. Give it your best shot. Give it your best shot. I took off. I could feel the friction of the air on my body as I rose and rose like some sort of Nike missile. As I got to the top of my jump, I made a fist and I swung as hard as I could. Pow! I hit him in the nuts. He crumpled to the floor, his eyes bulging out of his head, like a cartoon character who just hit his own thumb

with a hammer. He screamed in falsetto
for all to hear . . .

"Ow. Shit man. Time out! Nobody
walk here. My balls are here some-
where. Why did you hit me in the balls,
munchkin? Why did you hit me in the
balls?"

I gave it my best shot. Unfortunately,
it was to his balls, and they threw me out
of the game for an intentional foul. That
was the bad part. The good part was the
Indiana Pacers called and said I'm their
kind of guy.

After the game, everybody came
over to the house: the team, cheerleaders, friends. 549 was always the
hangout house. People just loved to
come over, and my mother would
cook for everybody. There must have
been fifty people there, and it was always okay that she stayed. Usually if
there was a party at a friend's house
and the parents were there, we would

figure out ways to get rid of them; not her. She was hip about it too. If there was a make-out party, she'd work the lights.

Billy and Janice in
Finian's Rainbow

Jesse and "Sammy" on *SNL*

CHAPTER 11

A few weeks after Dad had passed away, and everybody had gone, when it was just the two of us, Mom took me into my room in the back, closed the door and said, "Billy, listen. I want to talk to you about something."

"What, Ma?"

"When it's time, and it's going to come sooner than you think, you're going to get to go away to college. I don't want you to worry about that."

"Mom, I don't have to go away. I'll

215

get a job, and go to night school. I really don't have to go away."

"No, Billy. I want you to go. It's important for you that you go. Joel went away . . . Rip went away . . . I love you all the same. You'll have the same chance that they had."

"But Mom, the money . . ."

"Don't worry about that. I'll make it work, I promise you. I want you to go." And she became the greatest hero I will ever know in my life. My mom was fifty years old when my father died in front of her like that. Fifty. A woman who had to grow up, with a boy who couldn't help but grow up, and two others, who were still in college. She kept us together.

Uncle Milt came up with an idea to stage a big benefit concert for us at the Central Plaza, in December, just the way Dad had done for his players' families when they passed on. It was gigantic, all these great musicians in a nonstop show that went on for hours and hours. They raised something like five or six thousand dollars, but it disappeared with the guy who coordinated the evening. Shocking, somebody stealing this money from a widow and her kids. They never saw him again.

We had nothing. But like her father, Mom had "a plan." She started taking the train in from Long Beach into Manhattan round-trip every day. An hour each way, a tough commute for anybody. But when you're fifty and you've got that boulder to carry around, it's a little tougher.

Her plan was simple. She began to study at a secretarial school, to learn shorthand, typing and dictation so she could get a job as a secretary. She hadn't had a nine-to-five job since her days at Macy's in the thirties.

She'd had the toughest of all jobs, of

217

course, raising three children, but now it all depended on her, and she never complained. Mom was very matter-of-fact about life, this was how it was. I knew inside she was hurting, but she rarely let us see it. If she was weak, what would we think?

When we'd all be together, we'd go into Wing Loo, and when they'd ask, "How many in your party?" she would look them in the eye and say, "Four." I knew it was killing her, because it was killing me. I was always thinking, There's one empty chair.

When she got home from the City, I would do her homework with her. I would read her the sample business letters. I would do the dictation with her, and she would get it down in that crazy shorthand language. Then she'd have to type the letters for time on a typewriter. (Remember typewriters?) Get one thing wrong, or the keys stuck together, she'd have to start all over again.

"Time . . . Mom, that's only forty-eight words a minute. You have to get up to around sixty-five or seventy words per minute if you're going to compete for a job. Come on. Give it your best shot."

I would push aside my homework to help her with hers. After a few months of this, she was typing at seventy-five words a minute and she got a job, not just as a secretary, which would have been fine. She got a job as an office manager in Mineola, Long Island, at a Nassau County psychiatric clinic, which was perfect for me. Free samples. And during this dark time, she never complained, and she always had a sense of humor.

She'd come home from the clinic . . .

"Mom, you look tired."

"Oh, it's these damn schizophrenics. You have to bill them twice."

I graduated high school, and soon I would go away to college. Mom had put aside $2,500 so I could go. That may not seem like a lot to you, but she was only making $7,500 a year. I helped out a little bit too. I was going to Marshall University in West Virginia to be their next second baseman, because I could hit the curveball to right field. I was seventeen when I left to go away to college, a young seventeen in many ways, and a very old seventeen in a lot of ways. And I'd never been away from home.

I also never had the chance to have the "birds and the bees" speech with my dad. We never got to it—that almost mystical talk, when fathers hand their sons the baton of the relay race that is life. We did have the one talk about The Girl, but it wasn't the one I wanted . . . So right before I got on the plane at La

Guardia Airport, Eastern Air Lines, Gate 33, I had the birds and the bees speech with my mom.

"Billy, dear, before you go, about the girls—"

"Mom, I know."

"I'm so glad we had this talk."

We held on to each other for as long as we could as they announced my departure. I just didn't want to let go. It's tough to say goodbye to your heroes. But then there's a moment when you know you have to go. Something in your mind goes off, and it's suddenly okay. Because if you raise your kids right, they should go. I walked to the plane and never looked back, and then I heard three words that she would yell after me that would change my entire freshman year at school.

"DON'T WASH WOOL!"

*   *   *

221

I got down to Huntington, West Virginia, and the first day of school was a total disaster. They cancel the freshman baseball program because of a funding problem. This was years before freshmen could play varsity, so that was it, there would be no baseball for me. Suddenly, I'm simply a Jew in West Virginia. The only Jew in West Virginia it felt like sometimes. I had never felt hatred before.

A local restaurant wouldn't serve me after the counterman saw my Jewish Star hanging around my neck. Though my roommate, Michael, and I got along really well, I learned very quickly that there was a big world outside Long Beach.

I was shy and quiet without baseball, lonely, and still thinking about The Girl. But then I got involved with the campus radio station WMUL, and started spending time there doing my own show called *Just Jazz*. The jazz library at WMUL was nonexistent; Roy Clark was considered a jazz artist there. So, I called Uncle Milt, and he sent me some great albums, and I took a chance and wrote to the great John Hammond, the head of Columbia Records. Dad always had the nicest things to say about him, and I just decided to go for it. I told him, I was Jack's son, and Milt's nephew, and about Roy Clark. He sent me fifty of the classic Columbia records: Miles and Brubeck and Ella and Billie . . . a starter set of the masters. He also sent the Columbia catalogue (mail order, thank you Uncle Milt), with the opportunity to buy any album in it for a dollar. We exchanged a few letters, and he said to come in to meet him, maybe for a summer job. I'm sorry I didn't have the chance to thank him personally. He was a giant in the industry, and really helped me out.

Not only was it fun to be a deejay, but I found it so comforting to go into the station and just listen to jazz. I lived in the Pritchard Hotel in Huntington, nine blocks off campus, overlooking the train station. The school had rented two floors to serve as a dorm.

Michael and I had the smallest room on the eleventh floor. It was so tiny. It was either that, or that damn boulder was still too big. I took it with me every-place I went. Call me a slow healer but it hadn't even been two years, and, with the exception of my radio show, I had a tough time having fun.

Once a week I called home. Sundays now became our phone call day. After eight o'clock at night it was cheaper, so that's when I would call. I never told Mom it was hard for me, because I didn't want her to worry. I always tried to keep her spirits up, even though mine were falling. I don't think I ever fooled her, because my uncles would call and write, and Grandma, and my brothers of course, and my cousins even.

It was so great to get a letter. I felt like one of those actors in those war movies when someone brings a letter from home out to the battlefield: "Is that for me?" It taught me that family is not just the family that you grew up under the same roof with, it's your whole family. Then one day I got a package in the mail, which totally confused me because it was the only package I got all year that didn't have a salami in it.

It was from California: Hollywood, California. I didn't know anyone in California. I'd never been to California. The furthest west I'd ever been was Eighth Avenue at the old Madison Square Garden.

I opened it up and it was a book from Sammy Davis, Jr., who I had never met. Uncle Milt had been recording him. He did Sammy's first gold record, "Hey There" from *The Pajama Game*. A note from Uncle Milt was attached to the front of the book. It said he had written to Sammy about me. He told Sammy that he thought that I had something, but that I also had "the otherness." He signed it as he signed all his letters to me, "Keep thrillin' me, Uncle Milt."

I opened it up, and Sammy had signed the book to me. I could hear his voice as I read: "To Billy, you can do it, too. The best, Sammy Davis, Jr."

I came home for the summer of 1966, and got a job as a counselor in a day camp at the Malibu Beach Club in Lido Beach. One day after work, I was on the beach with my good friend Steve Kohut, and this really cute girl in a bikini with a fantastic walk goes by, and I said, "Who's that?"

226

"That's Janice Goldfinger," Steve said. "She just moved here."

I said, "I'm going to marry her."

We started dating, and I was in love. This was bigger and better than any feeling I'd ever had in my life. We were perfect together. She was beautiful in a way that was actually touching. I was only eighteen, and she was seventeen, but I wanted her forever. We were kids, but there was something about Janice that screamed at me, DON'T LET HER GO.

Her kindness was in everything she did. She was charming, and she was sexy, and she made me laugh. Most important, I didn't feel the otherness when I was with her. The day before I was supposed to leave to go back to Marshall, I decided not to. I knew if I left, she and I would never make it. Those long-distance romances never seem to work out.

I talked to Mom, and after she heard what was in my heart, she didn't try to change my mind. Mom would always tell me if she thought I was making a mistake. Not this time. I gave up my chance to play college ball for Marshall, and even though I knew it would be a better year, and it was a nice place, I just finally felt, Janice was too important in my life, and West Virginia was a little too "off-Broadway" for me.

So I enrolled at Nassau Community College in Garden City, Long Island, a two-year commuter school, to get my grades up, and as an elective, I took acting. That was it. I started acting in plays, and singing and dancing in musicals, even directing some. Nassau had a fantastic theater program, and I threw myself into it.

There was a great group of talented actors and actresses, with strong and creative teachers. I started to understand the process of doing real and honest acting work. We started our own summer stock company, which is how I got my Actors' Equity card. I got to direct and act in a production of *The Fantasticks* that starred my brother Rip as El Gallo. Rip had been singing professionally. He had been a regular chorus member on NBC's *Kraft Music Hall* and was getting parts in cabaret shows in New York.

The school was built on an old Air Force base, and we renovated one of the massive old airplane hangars into an indoor/outdoor theater. We could open the huge doors of the hangar and the audience would actually sit on the runway of the old airstrip. We would do straight plays and musicals, with a full orchestra, for crowds of over two thousand people. Once again, Rip joined me (along with Janice), as we starred in *Finian's Rainbow*. Janice played Susan the Silent and I was the Leprechaun, and when I sang

"When I'm Not Near the Girl I Love" to her, and we danced together, there wasn't a dry eye in the hangar.

It was a special time in my life. I knew that a career as a performer was what I wanted. I don't think I have ever stopped working on my skills since those great days at Nassau Community College.

Four years after I told Steve Kohut, "I'm going to marry that girl," I did. After Janice and I got married in 1970, we lived upstairs at 549 (Abe and Estelle had left). We lived above Mom for about four years, and it was so nice to have sex in the house with somebody who wasn't me. We've been married thirty-five years now, so I guess I made the right decision.

Fifteen years into our marriage and two daughters later (Jenny and Lindsay), in the middle of my career, I'm back in New York to do *Saturday Night*

Live. I went to my high school 20th reunion. It's 1985 and the Class of 1965 is together again.

I loved my friends so much. It was so great to see them, especially Michael Stein, David Sherman, Joel Robins, and David Beller. My face hurt from smiling the first half hour. And then I saw The Girl. Except now she was The Divorcee with The Bad Nose Job, The Fake Tits and The Fat Ass. Ain't life grand?

I went to the bar to get a drink to celebrate. Somebody taps me on the shoulder. I turn around. It was Harvey. Thirty-seven years old now, hairline on the run, and looking very upset.

"Are you mad at me? Because it was Joe's father. He was there. Billy, that's all I said. Joe, there's your father. I didn't mean to start nothing."

I said, "Harvey, I'm not mad at you." He didn't seem to hear me.

"Billy, you know, I feel so bad about

231

this. I see you in the movies now and TV. It's so great to see. I'm really—I'm proud of you, man. You're really doing it. Every time you're on TV, my friends are going, 'Hey, Harvey, Billy's on. He's your friend, right?' I go, 'No. He's mad at me.'"

"Harvey, listen to me. I'm not mad at you. I never was. It was my problem."

"You're not mad at me?"

"No," I said.

He looked at me with wonder, a huge sense of relief radiating out of his thirty-seven-year-old face, and then suddenly, he snapped . . .

"Fuck you then! For twenty years I thought you were mad at me and you're not mad at me? Pick up a goddamn phone! Let me off the fucking hook! And you know what else? You don't look so fucking Mah-velous! Fuck you!"

*   *   *

After the reunion, everybody came back over to the house, just like the old days. And my mother cooked for everybody, just like the old days. All of these friends, who had come into this house as young kids to listen to *The 2,000 Year Old Man* album or to watch a Yankee game or to listen to a great jazz album, were back, only now they were middle-aged people, showing my mother pictures of their kids. They were just as happy to see her as they were to see me. She even remembered their nicknames.

One of my friends is the head of medicine at a very big hospital in Southern California. He lectures around the world on these breakthroughs that he's making in oncology. He's a genius, and a very important man. When my mom heard what he was doing, she said, "Stinky, that's fantastic." We all laughed so hard. The living room was alive again.

So many stories in that house . . . so many stories. We grew up there. We measured our heights on the side of the den door in pencil every six months. We ate great food there. We laughed there . . . We made people laugh there. We were the Nairobi Trio there. We watched Sid Caesar there. I saw the Beatles there. We were Yankees there . . . We fell in love there. We brought our own kids there to get Mom's recipes . . . We mourned there. It was our house . . . So many stories.

East School
Long Beach N.Y.

Dear Mom,
    Did you have a nice ride in the ambulance?
Grandma has taken care of us better now well
she always does. How were you today. Last
night grandma gave us chicken and dumplings.
The class misses you very much and me
most of all. The house is very clean. In the morning
we make our beds and take our breakfast. Joe
only had a 100 temperature. Grandma couldn't
come because she was too tired.

                            Your loving son,

                                    Billy

P.S. I love you, mom

$\mathcal{T}$he last story would start on Halloween night of 2001. Once again, the entire country had the otherness. Our family was still reeling from the loss of Uncle Milt in late July, and Uncle Berns was having a very difficult time. He had fallen ill at Jenny's wedding the previous September, and Janice and I spent many months in New York, supervising his care. He was having trouble walking, and he had many other serious problems. I wouldn't let anything happen to him. He became my eighty-seven-year-old son. On September 4, of 2001, exhausted, we finally moved him and my Aunt Deborah into a brand-new assisted-living facility, which was just two blocks from the World Trade Center. Only a high school football field separated them.

A week later, the world changed. We were back in Los Angeles, paralyzed with fear, not only for him, but also for our younger daughter, Lindsay, who was living in New York. We were on the phone with Berns, watching the television coverage as the second tower fell. The phone went dead. I screamed a sound that had never come out of my mouth before. Berns was in a wheelchair, his legs had failed him months before, and I couldn't help feeling that the towers had fallen on his building.

Lindsay was living in the East Village, and watched the towers fall from the roof of her building. She had the same terrifying thoughts we had: Berns is there!

The only way we could communicate was to instant-message on our computers. She wrote, "I have to get to Uncle Berns," and the sweet-sounding tone went off, making the whole thing even more surreal . . .

I wrote back, "Stay where you are. We don't know what this is. There is another plane in the air."

Lindsay finally got through to the front desk of Berns's building and found out that the police and firemen had evacuated all the senior residents, and that they were safe.

The events of the day, and the terrible days after, were just overwhelming, emotionally, physically, spiritually. We knew our world would never be the same. A few weeks after that, one of our closest friends, Dick Schaap, the sports journalist, became terminally ill from complications following hip surgery. It was a dark time for us, the shadows were everywhere.

But on this Halloween night, the ghosts and goblins were just kids on the street as I passed them on my way to Game Four of the World Series. That was an odd Series, the Diamondbacks versus the Yankees. It was the only World Series that the country actually wanted the Yankees to win, just so something good would happen to our city after what had happened to us all a month and a half earlier. I was getting onto the West Side Highway just seconds from Ground Zero, near where I live now, and my cell phone went off. It was my brother Joel.

"Billy, listen. We have a big problem. Mom had a stroke."

"What?"

"I found her in the living room. The doctor said she's going to make a complete recovery, but it's bad. She's really confused. We're at the Long Beach Hospital Emergency Room so get here as soon as you can. All right? See you here. Bye."

Stunned by the suddenness and the fear of it all, we drove the hour and a half out to Long Beach. We got there as fast as we could. I met with the doctor. He said, Yes, indeed. She had had a stroke, but if you're going to have a stroke, this is the one you want to have. What the hell does that mean?

He showed me her X-rays. I saw the villain. He explained, as he pointed to the bleed, that it was in a very safe position in her brain. She would make a full recovery—"great"—but her left arm has been weakened badly but he thought it would come back—"great"—she's very confused right now, and that she's over there. He pointed to where she was, a male nurse attending her.

I saw her from the distance. Her left arm had been weakened to the point where it was hanging limply, but she knew that we would be coming. In the first aftermath of the stroke, she started to check out her body to see what this "opponent" had done to her. She saw that the arm was weak. She then took the sheet, and put it in her bad hand and held it as best she could. She evened the sheet off around her waist, so that when we saw her for the first time, we wouldn't know she had a problem. She was protecting us. When I realized what she was doing I said to myself, God, she's great.

"Mom . . . Mom, I'm here now. Janice is here. Rip is flying in. Joel's here. Everything's going to be great, Mom. I spoke to your doctor, he said you're going to make a complete recovery. Isn't that wonderful news?"

She looked at me with very confused eyes. I studied her face. I'd never thought of my mom as old. Even though she was in her eighties, her spirit was always so young. She looked beat up now, worn out, but still so valiant in her struggle to overturn what had just been done to her. She looked like she wanted to sit up and say, "Let's get the hell out of here." Instead, she spoke to me as if she was a little girl.

"My head hurts."

I was shocked, but couldn't let her see that. "I bet it does. I bet it does. There?"

"Yes," came the weak reply.

I massaged the back of her head as I held her good hand.

"I will always take care of you, Mom, always."

"Thank you," she murmured.

243

Then she stopped talking. No speech, just staring straight ahead. No speech the rest of that day and well into the next day. I ran to the doctor, anger and fear in my voice . . .

"Did you tell me everything? She's not speaking."

"Billy, calm down. Calm down. Your mom can speak if she wants to, but she doesn't want to right now. Her brain is making new connections, trying to figure out what happened to it. And right now, and it's a very normal feeling, she's angry."

He was right. She was furious that God had insulted her body this way.

"Well, how do I get her to speak?"

"Bill, with all due respect, I heard you tell her that you spoke to me, and that I told you she's going to make a complete recovery, which I believe she will, but she doesn't want to hear that now."

244

"How can I talk to her?" I asked.

"Just talk about everyday things . . . Try to engage her that way. Just talk about everyday things."

"Okay. I'm sorry, Doc."

He nodded sympathetically.

I went back into her room. She was staring at nothing. It was like someone had taken Mom and replaced her with a duplicate. It was her, but not really her . . . I wanted to yell, GIVE ME MY MOTHER BACK . . . I started to talk to her . . .

"Mom, this game last night was unbelievable. The Yankees are losing three to one, ninth inning, two out, O'Neill is on first, Tino's up, and he hits a home run. Ties it up. The Stadium went nuts! Then later, Jeter hits a home run and they win it."

And she suddenly said, "Well, it's

245

about time. Derek hasn't been doing anything."

My elation was short-lived. These strokes are nasty characters. They're mean. It's a mean illness. A little bit of progress like that, and then many steps back. Some days you'd have a smile on your face, and the stroke would know it, and it would slap your other cheek. It's a mean, cunning, nasty illness. It was so hard to go to the hospital.

I kept thinking about the first time she had been in this very same hospital. I was nine years old. It was right after we got the car. She had pneumonia, and they took her out the front door with the ambulance waiting in the driveway, the gurney rolling on the cement, all that noise. I stood in the driveway as she passed me wearing the oxygen mask, the weak wave goodbye.

"Don't worry. I'll be okay."

They put her into the ambulance, the sirens wailed, and she was gone. I was terrified. My mom was going to the hospital.

Terrified. Just the way I felt now.

And the day after she checked in, I called her up. It was a stormy day, very windy and pouring rain. I said, "Mom, I'm coming over to see you. I have a new routine, it's really funny. I want to make you laugh."

She said, "You can't come here, you have to be sixteen."

"So, I'll do it outside," I pleaded . . .

"No, it's pouring. Don't come."

I said, "Mom, you can't stop me."

I hung up and I ran the seven blocks to Long Beach Hospital. The courtyard of the hospital is a U shape, and in the front was a big garden area. Right in the middle was this young sapling tree, about five and a half feet tall, no branches, very frail. They had just planted it. It was held up by some yarn and some stakes, but in the wind and the rain of the day, it was bending over very easily.

I stood next to it, looking up because I saw Mom in the third-floor window sitting up in a chair, looking out. When she saw me in the wind and the rain, she was not happy. She looked down at me in horror, and mouthed her words, broadly, so I could see what she was saying . . .

"Billy, no. I told you not to come. Go home, Billy. Go home."

I shook my head, "No." I came to make her laugh. So I started doing cartwheels and round-offs, back flips . . . all the things I could do back then. And then I got an idea. I took a run and I slid headfirst into the mud like a giant Slip 'N Slide, and I stood up, my face covered with mud, because I wanted to look like James Dean in her favorite movie,

Giant. Again horror from the third floor.

"No, no. Crazy boy. You're a crazy boy. Go home. Go Home." She pointed furiously at me to leave . . .

I shook my head, "No" . . . I came to make her laugh.

Wiping the mud off my face, I remembered she loved Charlie Chaplin. Chaplin was her favorite of all time. I started imitating Chaplin as best I could walking around the tree, leaving Charlie's footprints in the mud. Then I got another idea. I started talking to the tree as if it were a beautiful girl, because Charlie flirted with everybody. And then I embraced it, and I bent the tree over, and stole a kiss just like Charlie would do.

I looked up. Mom was laughing, a big warm laugh, her shoulders shaking. She held herself, as if we were hugging each other. Then she mouthed . . .

249

"Go home."

I got my laugh. She blew me kisses in the rain, and I ran the seven blocks to the house, my Keds never once touching the concrete.

But now I stood by this very same tree, except now this tree was almost fifty years old. Its November branches gnarled and twisted like an old man's hands reaching up to the heavens as if to say "Why?"

I sat with her, holding her hand.

"Mom, remember when you had pneumonia, and I was outside in the rain? I did Chaplin in the rain. Remember that, Mom? You were so mad. Remember when I did Chaplin in the rain? Do you?"

Her eyes opened wide.

"You're Billy Crystal! What are you doing here?"

She didn't know me as her son.

These strokes are like bank robbers. They break into your vaults and steal the things that you treasure most, the things that are most valuable to you, your memories. They steal your life.

But then she rallied, like I knew she would. The arm came back. She got off the bed, started walking with a walker first and then a cane, then with nothing at all. And all of us stood there, the whole family rooting her on. She never complained and always had a sense of humor. One day, as she was walking down the hall with the nurse, she turned to us and said, "Don't just stand there, put up the hurdles."

I had to leave, just for three days, an event I couldn't get out of at the last minute. I flew to Seattle, to perform in a comedy concert. The first time for me alone onstage in fifteen years. Next morning after the show, I called her in

251

the hospital. Joel and Rip put her on the phone.

"Hello, darling. How did the show go?" She remembered . . .

"Mom, it went great."

And she always asks me technical questions. "How many people were in the house, dear?"

"Mom, it was a big joint. You know, it was like Radio City Music Hall. Do you remember Radio City, Mom?"

"Of course. We saw Danny Kaye in *The Court Jester* there."

"Yes, we did. Yes, we did," I said, tears of hope filling my eyes.

I went into great detail how the show worked for me, where the laughs had flowed, and she just simply stopped me and said, "Billy, dear, were you happy?"

"Yeah, Mom, I was."

"Well, darling, isn't that really all there is?"

She took my breath away . . . Words were difficult to come by . . . "Yeah. Mom, listen. I have one thing I can't get out of tomorrow, a big meeting in L.A. But I'm going to make the red-eye in. I'll be there Tuesday, Mom. We'll have breakfast together. What do you want me to bring you, Mom, you name it. Everything's going to be great. You'll see. Everything's going to—"

She stopped me again and said, "Billy, dear, please. Don't worry about any of that. Darling . . . I'll see you when I see you."

And that's the last time we spoke. The next day the bank robbers broke in again. This time they stole her.

The funeral was as it should have been. Her grandchildren spoke, Uncle Berns read a letter my dad had written

253

to him during the war, telling him how happy he was to be in love with her. Joel was funny, I was funny, and Rip sang. She rests next to Dad, and even in my sorrow, I found some comfort in the fact that they were together again, in their same bed positions, quiet and peaceful, just like I saw them every morning of those 700 Sundays.

So now I'm an orphan. Fifty-seven years old now and an orphan. I know people will say, "Come on, Billy. This is what happens to us. This is what happens to all of us at this point in our lives. This is how life works."

But do you know something? It has an odor to it. I don't know why I thought it would be easier this time. I was fifteen the first time. Fifty-three the second. The tears taste the same. The boulder is just as big, just as heavy, the otherness just as enshrouding.

The anger started to well up again.

254

But an omnipotent being once told me it's the hand I'm dealt. The cards I get to play.

We're at a table. I'm sitting across from "Him," and there are five cards spread in front of me.

I pick up the first . . . "Maybe five foot seven?" Oh come on.

I turn over the second . . . "Lose your father when you're fifteen." Can I get another card?

My third card . . . "Have your mother her entire life."

And the fourth . . . "Marry an incredible woman, have two beautiful daughters, and now your first granddaughter."

The last one . . . "Get to do what you've always wanted to do since you first made them laugh in the living room."

I hold the cards in my hand. He stares me down. I look at them one more time, but I don't really have to.

"I'm going to stick, and I'm going to raise you everything I have. What do you got?" I stare at him with confidence, waiting for God to make his move. He stares back. I smile. He folds . . . He can't beat me.

About a year before my mom passed away, it was a Saturday night in Los Angeles, very late, around 12:45 on a Saturday night, which actually makes it a Sunday. The phone rings and I panic, because when you're a Jew and the phone rings late at night, it means somebody's dead. Or worse, they want money. But no. It's Mom calling from the house.

"Mom, are you okay?"

"Yeah. I'm fine, dear."

"But Mom, it's three-thirty in the morning."

"I know. I just wanted to hear your voice, Bill. That's all. I woke up your brothers too, but I wanted to hear your voice."

"But you're okay?"

"Yeah. I just—I couldn't sleep. I've been having trouble sleeping, and I just couldn't sleep."

"Oh, really . . ." I softly said, nodding my head. Her honesty was disarming.

I'm an insomniac myself. I mean, I've been up since 1948. I wanted to find out why she couldn't sleep because somehow it might help me. But, really, I just wanted the conversation to keep going on, because these kinds of conversations with your parents are best when they're not just your parents, but they feel like they're your friends.

"Mom, why can't you sleep?" There was a pause, and then . . .

"Oh, I'm listening for you boys."

I knew exactly what she meant. The cry in the middle of the night, "Mommy, I have a fever." The nightmares, "Mommy,

257

there are pirates in the room!" Then as they get older, the sound of their cars pulling up in the driveway, the jingle of their keys in the front door lock, just so that you know that they're home safe. She was eighty-five years old now, alone in that house, her sons scattered across the country, but she was listening for us.

We sold the house. We had to. Without her in it, it really didn't make much sense to keep it. Somebody else owns it now, but it doesn't belong to them . . . because I can close my eyes and go there anytime I want.

EPILOGUE

7 00 Sundays is not a lot of time for a kid to have with his dad, but it was enough time to get gifts. Gifts that I keep unwrapping and sharing with my kids. Gifts of love, laughter, family, good food, Jews and jazz, brisket and bourbon, curveballs in the snow, Mickey Mantle, Bill Cosby, Sid Caesar, Uncle Berns and . . . "Consider the rose. Can you dig that? I knew that you could."

I've had a recurring dream. I'm in a car, a gray-on-gray Plymouth Belvedere, and I'm sitting up front because I still don't need legroom. And there's nobody else in the car, and the car is driving itself. I'm not scared because it seems to know exactly where it wants to go. Then suddenly, we're on 42nd Street between Lexington and Third, and we pass the Commodore Music Shop. And we pass the Commodore Hotel.

We pull up in front of Grand Central Terminal, and the car comes to a stop. The door opens and I get out, and I just follow the crowd, past the Oyster Bar, up the ramp into the Great Hall. Except this time, all the stars are real, and they're brightening up the heavens, and it's just so beautiful.

And the terminal is filled with men, and they're all dressed how I best remember Dad—white shirt, sleeves rolled up to just below the elbow, collar open, knit tie hanging. They're all fathers waiting for their sons.

I can't find him, in the crowd, but then I see him and he sees me, and he looks great. He doesn't look worried, he doesn't look upset, and he doesn't look mad. And we walk toward each other. There's no reason to run. There's plenty of time.

"Hi Pop."

He smiles that sweet little smile, puts his hand on my shoulder and simply says . . .

"What's lead?"

"Pb," I answer with confidence.

He nods his head . . . "Good, Bill, good." We look at each other; it's quiet. "Did you eat?"

And I hear the clatter of plates, the laughter of the family, the smell of soup and brisket and noodle pudding. Dad's eyes motion for me to turn, and there they are, all together again at the table . . . Grandma and Grandpa, Uncle Milt, Uncle Barney, Grandma Sophie, and now Mom and Dad, waiting for me to sit down and eat, and then it'll be time to go into the living room, and do a show.

I'll see you when I see you.

June 1963...our last
photo together

Joel, me, and Rip